Dream Catcher

Dream Catcher

Reflections on the Joseph Saga

RANDY L. HYDE

Foreword by John Killinger

RESOURCE *Publications* • Eugene, Oregon

DREAM CATCHER
Reflections on the Joseph Saga

Copyright © 2022 Randy L. Hyde. All rights reserved. Except for brief quotations in critical publications or reviews, no part of this book may be reproduced in any manner without prior written permission from the publisher. Write: Permissions, Wipf and Stock Publishers, 199 W. 8th Ave., Suite 3, Eugene, OR 97401.

Resource Publications
An Imprint of Wipf and Stock Publishers
199 W. 8th Ave., Suite 3
Eugene, OR 97401

www.wipfandstock.com

PAPERBACK ISBN: 978-1-6667-3068-5
HARDCOVER ISBN: 978-1-6667-2249-9
EBOOK ISBN: 978-1-6667-2250-5

JANUARY 19, 2022 3:38 PM

Dedicated to
Charley and Molly
in hopes that all their dreams come true

Contents

Foreword by JOHN KILLINGER | ix
Preface | xv
Acknowledgments | xvii
    PRIVILEGED SON | 1
    TWENTY PIECES OF SILVER | 9
    THE BLESSING OF THE LORD | 17
    THE LORD MADE IT PROSPER | 25
    DREAM CATCHER | 33
    PLENTY AND WANT | 41
    BROTHERS | 49
    THE BABY OF THE FAMILY | 57
    THE SILVER CUP | 65
    REUNION | 72
    WAGON TRAIN | 80
    FAVOR | 89
    THE BLESSINGS OF YOUR FATHER | 98
    INTENTIONS | 106
Bibliography | 115

Foreword

by John Killinger

I have noticed, since reading this book, a definite uptick in the number of dreams I now remember when I wake up. The experts say we dream many times a night but don't remember a majority of our dreams. Considering the importance of many of the things we dream about, that is a terrible waste, especially if one believes as I do that our dreams are sometimes more connected to overall reality than our waking lives are.

My wife and I disagree about dreams. She thinks they are accidently and largely unrelated to the actual needs and or events in our lives. She would probably agree with old Ebenezer Scrooge, who said in *A Christmas Carol* that the things he saw in the night were the product of some undigested bit of mutton he had eaten.

But I believe in the importance of dreams. Some of mine have been powerful reflections of what was happening in my life at the time, and have even pointed me to meaningful solutions to problems I was trying to solve. And at one significant point in my life, when I had made a move to a new position, a whole series of dreams proved invaluable in helping me to quell my anxieties.

I had been the pastor of a large, extremely busy parish on the West Coast, and had been lured away from that job by the offer of

FOREWORD

a distinguished professorship at an eastern university. I thought at the time when I accepted the professorship that it was a wonderful opportunity to have more freedom to read and write—two passions for which I had little time in the church—and to be freed of the constant, almost overwhelming pressure of a couple of thousand parishioners and their problems.

But I hadn't been away from the pressures very long before I became depressed because I missed them. I felt out-of-pocket, as if my life no longer counted for what it had once been worth. I did read, and I wrote a little, but not with a lot of heart. I had never known depression in my life, but now I thought I had a bad case of it.

I knew I needed help.

Of all the great psychologists, Carl J. Jung was my favorite. I liked his books. As a professor of literature, I had always valued his insights into the great myths and stories of the world. So I decided I would find a Jungian psychiatrist, somebody who had spent years studying Jung's work, and share my problem with that person. A pastor friend who kept a list of counselors by his phone told me about a woman who had a good reputation as a Jungian analyst. I phoned her and told her my situation. That was in early January. She said, "I'm sorry, but I couldn't possibly take you on, as I'm leaving in April for a year abroad and I never accept clients for less than a year."

I still laugh at the response I offered.

"But I'm not very sick," I said. "I'm still able to function. Couldn't you possibly work me into your schedule for the three months you have left?"

I think my insistence amused her. She finally relented, and I went for my first appointment.

The first thing she asked me after I was seated in the comfortable chair in her counseling room was whether I had had any significant dreams recently.

I couldn't think of any.

Foreword

"We'll be working with your dreams," she said. "Keep a pad by your bed. When you dream something, write it down. Then we can discuss what is happening in your inner being."

I thought that would put the quietus on the whole business.

But I did as I was told, and was surprised the first night that I did indeed have a dream, was able to wake up enough to scribble something on the pad, and quickly went back to sleep.

As I followed this process, I caught more and more of my dreams and remember them in more and more detail. Soon, at our weekly sessions, I was bringing five, six, or even eight or ten dreams along, all of which I had typed up the mornings after I scribbled some notes about them on my bedside pad.

I still have my copies of those dreams. The stack of paper is probably an inch thick.

At first, I was dreaming of unpleasant things. There was a lot of urinating and defecating in the dreams. I remember one in which I was coming out of the apartment building where my family and I once lived in Paris, France, and found the street outside flowing with feces that had bubbled up from the sewers. I couldn't go anywhere without wading through the muck.

I was almost embarrassed to tell my counselor these dreams, but she waved off my apologies.

"I have counseled a lot of ministers," she said. "Most of them have such dreams that have to be worked through."

Then, after a month or two, the dreams became more and more pleasant. Shortly before Easter, and a couple of weeks before my counselor was due to leave for Europe, I had a radiant dream in which I was in a beautiful garden near an underground spring from which clear water was gushing forth.

Even in my dream, I recognized this place as Eden, the biblical garden, and recalled from some book I had read that the word "Eden" meant "the source of many waters."

I had an impulse to fish, but I had only an old-fashioned fishing pole. From somewhere—remember, this was a dream—I plucked a big, fat, juicy worm. I attached it to the hook at the end of the line and cast it into the water.

Foreword

Wham!, a large fish immediately struck the bait and I pulled it out. Disengaging it from the hook, I laid it on the grass.

There was half a worm left, so I threw the line out again, and *wham!*, I caught another big fish!

I laid it beside the one I already had.

Now the bait was gone and the hook was bare. What the heck, I thought, this is only a dream, so I tossed it out again. Incredibly, another big fish grabbed the hook and I landed it and laid it beside the other fish I had caught.

The three of them formed a sort of triangle in the grass.

Without comment, after I had described this dream, my counselor rose from her chair and crossed the room to a bookcase. A few moments later, she found what she was looking for. She opened the book to a particular page and brought it over and laid it in my lap. I looked at the illustration on the page. It was a line drawing of three fish, laid head to tail as in my own dream. The description under the drawing said: "A symbol of ancient Christianity, a sign of fullness and joy."

It was almost Easter. I had dreamed about Easter in a very personal pictorial way, and suddenly knew that my quest for restoration of happiness was complete.

I had never been happier in my life.

May I tell one more story?

When I was sixteen, I always turned out the lights in my little attic room before going to bed and knelt at my bedside for prayer. One night, as I was praying, I became suddenly aware of a luminescent form a few feet away, at the end of the room. I stared in amazement. It was a spectral image of the angel Gabriel. Without asking, I knew who it was. I wasn't dreaming. I was quite aware that I was fully awake and this was happening. Gabriel didn't say a word. He just stood there for what could have been a few seconds or an hour and then simply disappeared. I can't explain it. I hadn't even been thinking about angels. But that one-time appearance became a rock to my faith and understanding for the remainder of my life.

FOREWORD

Years later, when I was a professor at Vanderbilt University, I was lying on the sofa in our den as my wife was preparing supper in the adjoining kitchen. I was puzzling about whether to accept an offer to become the pastor of a large church in another state. I was obviously in a state of bewilderment and anxiety, for I was contemplating a major change for me and my family. I did not want to make a mistake.

Then, totally unbidden, I had what I can only call a waking dream. I saw it all as if in a sleeping dream, but I was not asleep.

I found myself standing on a hill on the small Greek island of Mykonos, near a modest hotel where my son and I had spent a couple of nights while backpacking through the islands. I heard and saw a lot of commotion as people raced toward the harbor below, where a ship that resembled an ancient Spanish galleon was sailing in. I joined the crowd and was standing on the dock when the gangplank was lowered and the captain of the ship strode off. He was dressed in medieval armor, and looked exactly like Rembrandt's famous painting "The Man in the Golden Helmet."

The captain came directly to me as he was raising his visor. I was astounded, for I was looking into the face of Gabriel, the angel I had seen all those years before.

"Don't you know," he said, "that I've always been with you?"

That was all. He had always been with me.

The dream ended, but I never forgot it, or the words that were spoken to me. I knew Gabriel would be with me whatever I did, whether I made the move I was contemplating or not. It gave me the courage to make an important decision.

Dreams? Yes, I believe in them—heartily—and I believe they have an inestimable value in our lives.

This is why I think this book you are about to read is very important. It may center on the dreams of the biblical character of Joseph. But it reminds us again and again that we shouldn't ever take our dreams lightly. They come from and speak to the very deepest places in our souls.

So read this book. You will be glad you did.

Preface

It is my nature, when considering an important decision, to do my homework and prepare as best I can. I am not impetuous by nature, sometimes perhaps to a fault. My last automobile purchase came after more than eight months of research. Of course, taking a bit more time to save up for a down payment didn't hurt! Recently, my wife Janet and I needed to replace our upstairs windows and have some other light carpentry work done. Finally, after securing five estimates, in a minor tone of exasperation she said to me, basically, "We need to cut bait and fish!" In other words, "get 'er done!"

The idea of writing a book on the life of Joseph, the son of the Hebrew patriarch Jacob, came to me years ago. Why did I sit on it so long? Needless to say, as a full-time pastor, time constraints got in the way. At least, that is what I told myself, that there is little discretionary time in the ministry. Perhaps I subconsciously waited to see if someone else would do it first. Surely, a Hebrew scholar would have deeper insights than I, and would represent Joseph better. But while there may be volumes "out there" of which I have no knowledge, it seems to me that works on Joseph are a bit scant.

During the time in which I put off writing this book, I cannot say honestly that Joseph kept coming to me in my dreams. After all, I confess that, unlike Joseph—and my friend and mentor John Killinger, who writes the foreword to this book—I am not a great interpreter of dreams. Still, the idea of writing about Joseph just would not leave me alone, and from time to time he would visit me in my thoughts and ask why I had not yet attended to his life

PREFACE

story. So finally, now in retirement, I followed my wife's advice. The pages that follow are my fishing expedition!

Joseph's story is utterly fascinating, and if you will take the time to read the narrative found in the Book of Genesis, chapters 37 to 50, I do believe you will come away with a much greater insight into your own personal faith. The study/thought questions following each chapter, for personal or group consideration, are designed to help you do that as well.

It is my hope that this effort, which attempts to fill in some of the gaps not otherwise addressed by the original authors, will encourage you in your journey of life and faith. And who knows, it might even help you catch your own dreams as well.

Randy L. Hyde
Little Rock, Arkansas
2021

Acknowledgments

MY wife has been my companion and best friend for fifty-two years, a constant encourager to all my endeavors. She has participated in our peripatetic wanderings with a cheerful heart, and entered our various church communities with a desire to serve. That spirit is reflected, I hope, in these meditations on Joseph's faith adventures. Thank you, Janet, for your grace and love.

My former professor, John Killinger, remains a dear friend and mentor. I am grateful for his illuminating and personal foreword to this effort.

I offer a special thank-you to my dear friends Elizabeth and Aliou Niang. A former theologian-in-residence at First Baptist Church in Memphis, Tennessee (where I served a more than two-year interim) and now tenured professor at Union Theological Seminary in New York City, Aliou introduced me to Wipf and Stock Publishers, encouraged me as I shared with them my manuscript, and assisted me in preparation for publication. Elizabeth cheerfully edited my work with a remarkable eye for detail. This book would not have been possible without their friendship and help. I owe them immeasurably.

Privileged Son

*Now Israel (Jacob) loved Joseph more than
any other of his children . . .*

GENESIS 37:3

Perhaps you are familiar with the Dream Catcher of Native American lore. Thought to have originated with the Ojibwe people, the dream catcher is a handmade object based on a willow hoop on which is woven a loose net or web. It is then decorated with objects considered to be sacred, such as feathers and beads. If you've ever traveled west, no doubt you've seen them.

There is an ancient legend of a Spider Woman known as Asibikaashi. She was the caretaker for the tribe, and was known to keep evil spirits and bad dreams from reaching the children. Eventually, the Ojibwe Nation spread to the four corners of North America, and it became difficult for Asibikaashi to be present to all the children. What could they do when she wasn't available to help protect them? The mothers and grandmothers in the tribes wove magical webs for the children, using willow hoops and sinew. In their way of thinking, the dream catchers would filter out all bad dreams and allow only good thoughts to enter their minds. Once the sun rose, all bad dreams would disappear.[1]

---

1. https://bluefeatherspirit.wordpress.com

Dream Catcher

The fortunes of the ancient nation of Israel began with a dream, and with Joseph, the next-to-last son of Jacob, the Hebrew patriarch. Joseph was the original dream catcher of Israel. He didn't necessarily filter out all the bad dreams, we will discover as his story unfolds, but dream he did. And he could interpret dreams for others, a gift that both liberated him and got him into a great deal of trouble.

Are you a dreamer? I have dreams, as we all do, but I must admit they are pretty mundane in most respects. My mother liked to have us share our dreams around the breakfast table. Once we had all related ours, my dad, the down home Mississippi philosopher-poet, would always respond by saying, "Know what I dreamed? I dreamt I was awake, and when I woke up I found out I was asleep!" When it came to dreams, that's about as deep as it ever got in our family. So I tend not to spend much of my time trying to figure out what my dreams might mean.

That's not true of everyone, to say the least. My former professor and friend, John Killinger, has vivid dreams that have often found their way into his sermons and books as he interprets their meaning, not only for himself but for those with whom he shares the gospel. It is a rare gift, in my mind given to few, given to those who have more of a mystical side, perhaps.

Evidently, Joseph had the gift in spades. He didn't always know how to handle this gift appropriately, especially when he was young, creating an ever-deepening rift with his brothers. We are told that "Israel (the name given to his father Jacob when he wrestled with God on the banks of the river Jabbok) loved Joseph more than any other of his children (37:3)." Despite his privileged status in the family, Joseph vexed his father, not only with his dreams but with his eager willingness to interpret them, even when nobody else wanted to hear about them.

You see, it is one thing to interpret dreams. It's quite another when you make yourself out to be the hero of all your own narratives; and that is exactly what the adolescent Joseph did. It wasn't entirely his fault. Joseph came by this naturally. After all, his father Jacob was a dreamer too.

PRIVILEGED SON

Years before, when Jacob fled the wrath of his brother Esau after cheating him out of his birthright, Jacob fled to Haran where his mother Rebekah had family. Perhaps they would be sympathetic to Jacob's plight since Jacob's mother, their kinswoman, had been the schemer who put him up to it in the first place. Along the way, Jacob spent the night, using a stone for a pillow. As he slept, he dreamt of a ladder reaching from earth all the way up to heaven, with the angels of God descending and ascending upon it (Gen 28:10–12).

Seeing this as a sign from God, Jacob declares that this place—a place to be known thereafter as *Bethel*, which means *sanctuary*—is "none other than the house of God, and this is the gate of heaven!" (Gen 28:17). Jacob believes that his dream is nothing short of a gift from God, and he uses it as encouragement for the journey before him.

And could it be that years before, when Jacob's grandfather Abraham heard the Lord say to him, "Go from the land of your fathers," that it was also in a dream? If so, we should not be surprised that Joseph would be a dream catcher. It is in his blood and in his bones. A dream catcher is all he can be, and interpreting dreams is all he can do.

When we first meet Joseph, he is seventeen years old. Do you remember seventeen? It is a very natural thing for seventeen year-olds to be totally self-absorbed. In fact, parents of teenagers could tell you that having a seventeen year-old might be theologically construed as God's divine punishment upon them. Added to this is that we are told Joseph is the favorite, privileged child of his father Jacob. It makes up a perfect mixture for volatility.

This is how the explosion comes about . . .

Being as young as he is, Joseph is confined basically to domestic chores as a helper to the sons of two of his father's wives. What we know of Joseph suggests that he used his situation as an opportunity not to do much in the way of labor while keeping an eager eye on his brothers in order to catch them in doing less than they should do. Joseph observes their work ethic (or lack thereof, at least from his perspective), and when their behavior is not what he thinks it ought to be, he rats on them. As the scriptures put it, "Joseph brought a bad report of them to their father" (Gen 37:2). We are not told what Jacob does about it, but it isn't hard to imagine the resentment this caused among the brothers. That's the first part of the mixture: the building resentment. And, it is the perfect introduction to an explanation of the family's dysfunction.

The second part of that volatile mixture has to do with Jacob's love for his son Joseph. Pure and simple, Jacob loves Joseph more than his other sons, and makes no bones about it. This is not an isolated dynamic. It happens in many families, even today. In fact, I have been told by one of my older brothers—who shall go unnamed!—that mom loved me best. I don't think it was true, but my brother evidently believed it, at least at one point. Otherwise, he wouldn't have ever brought it up.

In Jacob's case, it was quite true. He held more affection in his heart for Joseph than he did for his other sons. We can see why, even if we don't agree with it. They had so much in common, Jacob and Joseph, and the father evidently does nothing to hide this fact. Not only that, Joseph is the firstborn son of Jacob's much-beloved wife Rachel, who died giving birth to Benjamin, Joseph's younger brother.

And so, as a sign of his affection for his son Joseph, Jacob gives him *the* coat. You are familiar, no doubt, with Joseph's coat. Even those who know little of scripture are aware of it, if for no other reason than because of Andrew Lloyd Webber's *Joseph and the Amazing Technicolor Dreamcoat*. It is referred to as a coat of "many colors." That may not be a completely accurate interpretation since the meaning of the Hebrew is a bit garbled at this point. It might have been that the robe Jacob made for his son had special sleeves. Regardless of the original meaning, one thing is for certain: the coat is indeed special (certainly not off the rack!), given only to Joseph, and was the kind that was generally worn only by royalty, meaning the person who wore it would not be required to do menial labor. No doubt he paraded around in it like a cocky little rooster, throwing his privileged status in the faces of his older brothers.

Privileged Son

Can you feel the bitterness growing deeper on the part of Jacob's other sons?

Joseph is special and Jacob is partial. But why should we be surprised? The same was true with Jacob and his mother Rebekah. This is a family that simply does not know how to behave other than in a dysfunctional way, and now their misbehavior is being repeated in further generations.

However, the point of the narrative is that this dysfunction is what sets up the story line. The family dynamic is what drives the drama, and the dreams are the catalyst for how it all unfolds.

A story such as this can only tell us so much. There's a sense in which, if we are to understand it, we have to read at least somewhat between the lines. Let's do that for a moment, shall we? Imagine the conversations between Jacob and his privileged son Joseph. From the beginning Joseph would have known that his mother Rachel was Jacob's favorite wife. It is even quite possible that Jacob has recounted for Joseph the story of how he finally was able to take Rachel to be his betrothed, but only after being fooled by his father-in-law Laban into first marrying the older Leah. It stands to reason, then, that Rachel's son Joseph would be Jacob's preferred as well. Wouldn't Jacob want Joseph to have what he never had? Wouldn't Jacob want Joseph to be a dreamer too, just as he had been? Wouldn't Jacob whisper in Joseph's ear, so the other brothers could not hear, the special plans and hopes he had for his privileged son?

Joseph had probably been told by Jacob of the dream at Bethel, of the wrestling match at the river Jabbok, of how he schemed over the years to outwit his father-in-law Laban. He may have been merely seventeen, and probably was not prone to want to do much in the way of labor, but Joseph by this time had learned how to get by with his wits, as had his father Jacob. So when he dreams, he uses his dreams as the means to show his superiority over his brothers.

God had made it clear to Jacob that he was to be the progenitor of a great nation first promised to his grandfather Abraham. Surely it was not God's intention that any of Jacob's other sons would be the ones to lead Israel into the future. They didn't have what it took to do such a thing. And though Jacob loved Benjamin too, if for no other reason than his beloved Rachel had died giving birth to him, the older of the two, Joseph, would be the one to continue the spiritual legacy of this soon-to-be great nation (see Gen 49:27). All his life Joseph has been told he was special, that not only did his father Jacob have great plans for him, but God did as well.

Pretty heady stuff for a seventeen year-old.

A consideration of Joseph's older brothers throwing him into a pit will come at a later time, but for now let's look at an observation by Frederick Buechner. He says, no doubt with tongue in cheek, that if they had been brought to trial they would have been acquitted in any court in the land.[2] Nobody would have blamed them for what they did. That's how deep was the resentment in the family of Jacob, son of Isaac. The tension was so thick, it was just waiting for something to happen to cause an eruption.

We shall learn that the point of the story reveals God's weaving of a slow and patient purpose in the midst of all this drama. The interesting thing, however, is that throughout this narrative God is rarely mentioned, at least by name. As Barbara Brown Taylor puts it, "By the time he (Joseph) arrived on the scene, God had become silent. Not absent, just silent."[3] The picture we get of God is one who works behind the scenes, allowing God's children to behave as they wish, then taking the consequences of their behavior and working out the divine purpose in all of it.

That's strange, if not contradictory, when you consider that just two generations before God took the initiative with Abraham and told him to take his family and possessions and get out of Dodge. God had other things in store for Abraham and his offspring. And there is that story of the day, when camped by the oaks at Mamre, Abraham and Sarah are visited by the three strangers representing the Spirit of God. And what about God's demanding

---

2. Buechner, *Peculiar Treasures*, 77.
3. Taylor, *Gospel Medicine*, p. 116.

that Abraham sacrifice his son Isaac? God seems to be quite actively involved when it comes to Abraham.

And there was the aforementioned wrestling match at the river Jabbok between Jacob and the messenger of God. Didn't the all-nighter leave Jacob with a permanent limp? Yes, it did, but that was also when God changed Jacob's name to Israel and assured him he would continue the promise first given to his grandfather Abraham, the promise of a great nation.

But that's not how God chooses to relate to Joseph. God appears to leave him to his own devices, and right now, as a seventeen year-old, Joseph doesn't have a lot to work with. Except, Joseph has his dreams. He does have his dreams.

We all dream. And we all, to some degree or another, have experienced some form of dysfunction in life, whether it is a struggle with one's family or a struggle with one's faith. And remember: we were all seventeen once.

But one lesson we learn from Joseph's story is that in the able and grace-filled hands of God, even the volatile mixture of resentment and hatred and immaturity experienced in the household of Jacob can be brought into harmony with the final purpose that God ordains. And if God was willing to do that for Jacob and Joseph and their family, will God not be willing to do the same for you and me?

Ponder that question, if you will, and in the meantime we will wish for you pleasant dreams.

Study/Thought Questions

1. To you, are dreams simply a subconscious manifestation of sleep, or do they carry substance and meaning?
2. Do you seek to interpret your own dreams, or have you ever consulted someone else about them?
3. Would you consider yourself to be a mystical person?

4. Like Joseph, have your dreams ever resulted in difficulty or troubles? If so, why/how?
5. Like Jacob, do you think of your dreams as gifts from God?
6. Have you ever witnessed or experienced parental favoritism? How did it affect you?
7. Role-play a conversation between Jacob and Joseph and discuss how this affects you emotionally.
8. Barbara Brown Taylor says, "By the time he (Joseph) arrived on the scene, God had become silent. Not absent, just silent." Do you agree or disagree?
9. The author says that "in the able and grace-filled hands of God, even the volatile mixture of resentment and hatred and immaturity experienced in the household of Jacob can be brought into harmony with the final purpose that God ordains." Do you agree or disagree?

Twenty Pieces of Silver

"What profit is it if we kill our brother and conceal his blood?"

~ GENESIS 37:26 ~

History points out that it's not necessarily the crime that gets you, it's the cover-up. Just ask certain presidents or presidential wanna-be's, CEOs and other various forms of politicians and industry leaders who have tried and failed to get away with their misdeeds.

And preachers. Don't forget the occasional preacher—usually of the mega-church variety—who thinks he (it is usually a *he*) is above it all. And when he is caught with the proverbial hand in the cookie jar, he thinks he can piously lie his way out of it. In truth, there is no way to lie, piously or otherwise, and survive it. It is the lie, the cover-up, that will catch up to you sooner or later.

Case in point, the brothers of Joseph.

Joseph doesn't seem to have the same feelings of hatred toward his brothers that they have toward him. Perhaps his arrogance—or naivete, possibly—shields him from such petty feelings. He seems eagerly, if not readily, willing to accept his father's "invitation" to pay a visit to his brothers. But then, he has the advantage over his brothers. His father Jacob obviously loves him more than the others, has given him little or no responsibilities when it comes to work, and has provided him with *that* coat . . . you know, the one that connotes royalty. Joseph struts around the compound like a little prince while the others are supposed to bow down as if they were his servants.

It is bound to come to a head, and it doesn't take long. Jacob sends his favorite son on a mission to check on his brothers who are tending the family herds. It is not a little hike that can be completed before lunch. It turns out to be a trip of about fifty miles, so think of how long it might have taken Joseph to walk or ride such a distance.

The sons of Jacob are tending the family flocks near Dothan, having moved up from Shechem, a distance of about fifteen to twenty miles. Evidently, they are on a hillside, for from a distance they can see Joseph coming. That's when the scheming begins.

Going back to our presidential misdeeds example, despite the best efforts of Bob Woodward and Carl Bernstein we may never know all the ins and outs of how the Watergate burglary was first put together (or the ensuing coverup). But the writer of this biblical narrative is quite clear about how it all took place. "Here comes the dreamer," the brothers say to one another. They don't even call Joseph by his name. "Here comes *the dreamer.*" They see him approaching from the south, walking along as if he has no care in the world. Their father Jacob has made it quite clear that because he is special, Joseph is not to do any real work. Why would he be coming to them now? Probably to take back another bad report of their behavior. Their resentment boils over and they say to one another, let's kill him.

It will be a few minutes before he reaches them. "How shall we do it?" they ask one another. Not if, but how. They have the weapons. No shepherd could do his work without the means of warding off wild animals, natural enemies of the flock. They could pierce him through with a sword and he would bleed out in no time. Cut his throat perhaps. Or they could strangle him. Stoning would work. He could possibly suffer a long time if they were to do that. They wouldn't be opposed to a good stoning; their hatred runs that deep.

Twenty Pieces of Silver

That's when the elder brother Reuben steps in. He's thinking of his father and the impact this would have on him. Subsequent conversations between Jacob and his sons reveal less than warm relationships (see Gen 43, for example), but we catch an occasional glimpse of members of Jacob's family thinking of someone other than themselves. This is a case in point. "Let us not take his life. Shed no blood," he says to his brothers. "You see this pit? Let's throw him in there." His plan, evidently, was to rescue Joseph and take him back home to his father. But when Reuben's back is turned they sell Joseph to a group of traveling salesmen known as Ishmaelites, getting twenty pieces of silver for their troubles.

I am curious about a couple of things. If we had not known that their first impulse was to kill Joseph, we might think they threw him into the pit just to scare him into some sense of reality. They're sick and tired of Joseph, of his immaturity, his fanciful dreams, and of their father's obvious favor toward him. They're resentful of his being treated like royalty (remember: he even has the coat to prove it) while they labor away every day. On the face of it, we might think they're just trying to teach their little brother a lesson. But no, according to the biblical narrative, they really do intend to kill Joseph. The pit is Reuben's idea, an effort to stall for time until he can manage to get Joseph out and bring him back to his father. If Reuben had not suggested that they throw Joseph in the pit, they probably would have ended his life right then and right there.

But throw him in the pit they did, and immediately—and quite casually and nonchalantly, it seems—they sit down to have lunch. I rather doubt that Joseph took this sitting down, don't you? "Okay, fellas, the joke's over. You can let me out now. Reuben, Judah, Simeon . . . this isn't funny! Let me out of here! Let me out!" And all the while, they sit there munching on their sandwiches. Occasionally they look at one another, and with a shrug of their shoulders take another bite of lunch.

Another thing that has me curious . . . Eventually, they sell Joseph for twenty pieces of silver. There are ten brothers, a nice, even split. The youngest, Benjamin, is back home, too young to be involved in all this. Besides, as the second son of Rachel who probably looks up to his brother Joseph, he would never have gone in on the whole deal anyway. If he had been old enough, he would have run to his father and told him what was going on. There are ten brothers in on this plot to sell Joseph to the Ishmaelites.

How are they going to split the money? There are twenty pieces of silver. Did they divide their take evenly, two pieces per brother? Probably so. But remember: only eight of the sons came from Jacob's wives, Leah and Rachel. Four were the offspring of servants. Were they considered by the other brothers to be legitimate? Would the silver be shared equally with them? When they return home, with their grisly story of how Joseph had been torn apart by a wild animal, do they share their bounty with their sister? Of course not. Do they cast lots for the leftovers? Who knows. Did the blood money stain their hands? You can be certain of that.

Meanwhile, back home, Jacob is oblivious to what is going on, obviously. But then, Jacob seems to be blind about a lot of things. Based on what he has observed, Jacob had to realize the enmity between Joseph and his older brothers. To send him to them, so he might bring back a report on their well-being, was foolish and shortsighted in the least. Joseph had already brought a "bad report" on some of his brothers, the offspring of two of Jacob's wives. Did Jacob really think he would do anything differently this time, especially with Joseph's penchant for lording it over his brothers?

And when the brothers, a few days after telling Jacob his son Joseph is dead, began wearing newly-tailored suits, didn't Jacob become suspicious? Didn't he notice the new, expensive ring on Zebulon's finger? Where did they get the money for such extravagances? Terence E. Fretheim, in the *New Interpreter's Bible*, says you have to wonder about Jacob's motivation. Then he asks, "Is this the naive, loving father (the giver of the coat) who hopes that the brothers can work things out?"[1]

Do you know Jacob's story? How he and his mother Rebekah cheated his older brother Esau out of his birthright? How he escaped to Haran, where he lived all those years being taken

---

1. Fretheim/Keck, *New Interpreter's Bible*, Vol. I, p. 599.

advantage of by his father-in-law Laban, yet all the while scheming to overcome Laban's trickery with a plan of his own, if for no other reason than he loved Laban's daughter Rachel so much he was willing to wait and labor so he could have her hand in marriage? How, after finally escaping the clutches of Laban, he wrestled with the messenger of God at Jabbok and gained the eventual forgiveness of his brother?

Naive is not exactly a word that comes to mind when one thinks of Jacob. *Schemer*, yes indeed. *Trickster* (that is the meaning of the name Jacob)? Without a doubt. Naive? No.

Something doesn't feel quite right here.

Centuries later, in one of his encounters with the Pharisees—this time partnered with their political enemies the Sadducees—Jesus is once again put to the test. If he is as powerful as some people think, why doesn't he show them a sign from heaven as proof of his spiritual abilities? Jesus doesn't fall into their trap, of course. He says to them, "When it is evening, you say, 'It will be fair weather, for the sky is red.' And in the morning, 'It will be stormy today, for the sky is red and threatening.' You know how to interpret the appearance of the sky," he says to them, "but you cannot interpret the signs of the times" (Matt 16:1–4).

Jesus could have just as easily been talking to Jacob, couldn't he? How could Jacob be so blind, yes, so *naive* (!?), as to send his son Joseph into the hands of his older brothers who have already made known their hatred of him? Couldn't Jacob figure out what was going on under his own roof? Something just doesn't feel right about this.

But the uneasiness we feel as this drama gets more and more tense is nothing compared to the festering resentment and hatred his brothers feel for Joseph. We can't help but wonder how brothers—*brothers!*—could have such hatred in their hearts for one of their own. But remember that, while they all share the same father, that is not true of their mothers. They are but *half*-brothers, and spread apart by time and years. And who knows what kind of influence their respective mothers might have had upon them. Don't you think there could have been jealousy among Jacob's wives, not to mention the servants who gave birth to four of the brothers, jealousy over his affection and attention? If so, it stands to reason they would share it with their sons.

There are twelve brothers in the household of Jacob, all told, and they might not have had as much in common as we might think. The affection we feel for our siblings is evidently not operative in the family of Jacob, at least when it comes to Joseph.

This story could have turned out differently. Let's do a bit of imagining for a moment. Let's suppose the Ishmaelites (who, by the way, are also the sons of Abraham . . . did you pick up on that?), let's suppose they had not come along and Reuben was successful in freeing Joseph from the pit. What if it had happened this way . . . Reuben, being the oldest son of Jacob, and answerable to his father for Joseph's well-being, takes his little brother home. As the two are walking, Reuben has a long heart-to-heart with Joseph, tells him how his immaturity and dream interpretations have made his brothers angry enough to want to kill him; that when they get home, not only will Joseph not speak a word—*not a word!*—of what happened at Dothan, he will also quit his foolish behavior and start acting with more concern for the well-being of his siblings. In other words, it's time for Joseph to grow up. Do you think Joseph would have complied?

Perhaps. But we wouldn't have had much of a story, would we? There would be little if any redemption in it, no cause for forgiveness, no drama to set up the narrative of how the Israelites eventually found their way to Egypt. In fact, there wouldn't have been a story at all, and every narrative found in scriptures that follow after the Book of Genesis would have been changed completely.

So think about it, if you will. Everything—*the entire history of the world*—is affected by what happened that day in Dothan.

Look back over the meanderings of your own life. Chances are, your journey has been filled with crossroads. You had to make a decision here, take a road that went there. You were faced with deciding what you would do and where you would go, whether it was which college you might choose or the person with whom to spend the rest of your life; or not to choose any one at all. What job or profession did you pursue? Where did you decide to live? Think back on all that and realize that the determination you made at all those different and various points in your journey of life have brought you to this moment right here and right now.

Your story may not be as dramatic as Joseph's. Frankly, I hope it isn't. You probably agree. But it's been dramatic enough, hasn't it? Looking back, you can see how God took those decisions you made—some good, some not so good—and worked with them to establish the pattern, the framework, the tapestry of your life. There is a lot of redemption in that, and only God can do such a thing. Only God can do it.

Years ago, a friend of mine went on a mission trip to Africa. On Easter Sunday afternoon he decided to play touch football with the others who accompanied him on the journey, and during the game fell and broke his arm. The break was set by a doctor who was available in the area, but unfortunately the physician did not do it correctly. When my friend returned to the States he had to undergo a second surgery, during which his arm was re-broken and set again.

Not long afterwards, we were having lunch. I had to assist him with his crackers and other meal paraphernalia, and he apologized for the trouble. When I told him it was no bother, he said to me, "You know, I've heard people say that when they went on a trip like this God had directed them to do it. Well, let me tell you, I'm not going to put this on God. I've got nobody to blame but myself!"

There's a lot in all our lives for which we have nobody to blame but ourselves. But God doesn't leave us alone to face the consequences of our own actions. God has a heart of redemption whereby God takes our good deeds, as well as our mistakes, all the things we do and fail to do, the roads taken and not taken, and works with them until something good—something redemptive and good—takes place.

And that is true even when somebody gets thrown into a pit or Somebody gets put on a cross, all for a few pieces of silver. It's just the way God works. Don't ask me how. I'm not even sure I can always tell you why. I can only affirm that it is so, and I hope you can do the same.

And I hope it is enough, don't you?

Study/Thought Questions

1. The brothers refer to Joseph, not by name, but as "the dreamer." What do you think is the significance of that?
2. What do you think drove the brothers to such a level of hatred that they schemed to kill Joseph? Are there underlying factors not obviously stated in the biblical narrative?
3. Do you agree with the author when he suggests that Jacob is oblivious to the situation? If so, why do you think that is?
4. Do you think the family dynamic of multiple mothers has anything to do with the family's dysfunction?
5. The author says the entire history of the world is affected by what happened that day in Dothan. Do you agree?
6. The author refers to the "meanderings of life." Have you ever looked back and wondered how your life might have been different had you made other decisions?
7. To what extent has God not left you alone to face the consequences of your own actions?

The Blessing of the Lord

*His master saw that the LORD
was with him . . .*

୶ GENESIS 39:3 ଚ୶

So far, the story of Jacob—at least the part that includes Joseph—is pretty straightforward. We are told of how Jacob favors Joseph, if for no other reason than he was the firstborn of Jacob's late, beloved wife Rachel. We read of the enmity on the part of his brothers, not only because of Jacob's partiality toward Joseph, but also due to Joseph's dreams that place him in a position of authority and superiority over his brothers.

Rather than kill Joseph, which was their first impulse, they put him in a pit and then sell him to a group of traveling merchants who take him to Egypt and put him on the open slave market. They had paid twenty pieces of silver for Joseph. Maybe they can not only recoup their costs but make a healthy profit as well. They are businessmen after all.

So far, in this dramatic story, there is no mention of God. Until now. If we didn't know better, we would think that God has been watching this unfolding drama from the sidelines and has chosen not to intervene in the various skirmishes between Joseph and his brothers. God is biding time until there is an opportunity to make God's presence and purpose known.

Or, there is no effort on the part of Jacob's family to acknowledge God's presence or purpose in anything they do. That would especially be true, it seems, of Jacob's sons. When one is angry enough to provoke murder, it can easily be said there is no consideration of the divine.

The opportunity has now come for God to make an entrance. It is when Joseph is taken to Egypt and placed in the home of Potiphar, the captain of Pharaoh's guard, that Joseph really begins to come into his own. Somewhere, along the way, Joseph finally decides to grow up and be a man instead of an adolescent, immature dreamer. The writer of this story tells us, without any equivocation, that all this has come about in this manner because Joseph is blessed by the Lord. And that is key, not only to this portion of the story, but the whole of it as well. In fact, it is the underlying premise to everything we read in this fascinating narrative.

When our eldest grandson reached the same age as Joseph, as we are first introduced to him in the Book of Genesis (chapter 37), we counseled his mother, our daughter, about how best to deal with his adolescent behavior on the occasions when she would call and complain about him (we've had the opportunity to discuss this with other parents of teenagers as well). Our counsel was, and still is—as his younger brother has now come to this age—that as is true with many things, this teenage behavior will pass, as will her angst about it. They can pray that one day their sons will become good and productive adults. All they can do at this point is to remain faithful, try with all their might to be patient, and give their children the best guidance they can provide. But ultimately they must place their young ones into the hands of God.

If Joseph's story can be trusted, God is indeed good for it. It happened with Joseph, though it seems that it took being thrown into a pit and then taken into slavery to do it, but somewhere along the way Joseph did indeed grow up. At this point in the narrative, all credit for this is given not to Joseph but to the Lord.

Speaking of his slavery . . . there is no reason to think that Joseph's experience was like the nineteenth-century slave markets in the South. For example, chances are he was not shackled.

The Blessing of the Lord

Recognizing the futility of running away, he had probably used his considerable charm in convincing the Ishmaelites who had bought him from his brothers at Dothan that he was not a threat to attempt an escape. He had accommodated himself to the idea that he would be sold—to somebody. Perhaps it would go easier for him if he cooperated with his owners, that as a result of his cooperation they would be rather choosy as with whom they would do their business.

They take him to an open-air market where such transactions usually took place. Potiphar has been looking for some household help, someone he could trust to help manage his business interests. He spies Joseph and inquires of the Ishmaelites as to his availability. Yes, he can be procured, they tell him, for a certain price, of course. How much? We're not told what it is, but it's a safe guess that they settle on what is considered by both parties to be a relatively fair exchange. One thing we can be certain about: it was for more than twenty pieces of silver. Got to make a profit, don't you know! Once the transaction is completed and all the required papers are signed, young Joseph finds himself entering the next phase of his life.

How do you think you might have felt in those circumstances? Joseph would have been perfectly justified in playing the game of "Poor Me." But he doesn't. In fact, there are other places in his story where he faces problems, and does so with a faith that belies all that has happened to him. How could Joseph be so strong when confronted with these difficulties, especially after having been portrayed earlier in such an unfavorable light?

We may have the answer, but it will require us to once again read between the lines. Before anything else is said of Joseph, we are told that the Lord is with him. The timing of that statement is crucial. After being sold, but before he takes up his duties in Potiphar's household, God takes the initiative in providing his divine blessings to Joseph. Up to this point, if Joseph's story had been found in an ancient novel rather than in the Bible, we wouldn't have had any clue whatsoever that God had anything to do with any of this. It is not until the story is located in Egypt that we hear of God's involvement in the life of Joseph. It is good to know that Joseph doesn't have to go through this experience alone. "The LORD was with Joseph," we are told, "and he became a successful man" (Gen 39:2).

What does that mean, *successful*? It could be a reference to money. That's generally how we measure success, is it not? But I don't think that is what is meant in Joseph's case.

Really good and faithful employees are hard to find, and when you do it's important to reward them and keep them as happy as possible. At least, that has been my experience. As a senior pastor of five congregations, I have spent a great deal of time hiring staff, especially support staff; that is, those who work in the office. Frankly, with some, I can't even recall their faces, and in some cases have forgotten their names, if for no other reason than they didn't stay very long. But when staff commit to the church's vision, and have the maturity to hold the church's best interest at heart, the church—not to mention the pastor!—is blessed. Good and loyal employees are hard to find, and keep.

But Joseph wasn't an employee. He was a servant, bought and paid for. So when it comes to Joseph, what do we mean by the term *successful*? Can one be a servant and be successful at the same time? The answer to that question depends on the definition, doesn't it?

I think of a word that is generally not considered to mean the same thing as success, but which, I believe, definitely applies in Joseph's situation. The word is *trust*. Evidently, it did not take long for Joseph to gain the trust of Potiphar, to the extent that Potiphar had little or no worries about anything in regard to his household or his business. Joseph, his trusted assistant, takes care of everything.

Potiphar comes across in this story as a fair and just person. He recognizes Joseph's worth and rewards him accordingly. Just exactly how, we aren't sure. We are not told what *success* means when it comes to Joseph. But evidently, Potiphar thrives under Joseph's care, so his kindness toward Joseph may have been due directly to the fact that Joseph has brought prosperity to his household.

The Blessing of the Lord

Joseph is the kind of servant who manages everything. He's an office manager, secretary, and right-hand man all in one; an executive assistant, if you will. He is so efficient, in fact, that Potiphar has no real need. The final statement of our passage, speaking of Potiphar, says that "he had no concern for anything but the food that he ate" (Gen 39:6).

Do you find that to be a rather odd thing to say, a strange way of putting it? "He had no concern for anything but the food that he ate." What are we to make of that? Does this mean he has a lack of interest in anything else? Has Potiphar become so dependent on Joseph and his abilities that he has become lazy and thinks only of his next meal? Does that lethargy (that's the word for it, isn't it? *lethargy*) include his own wife? We will see very soon that her attention is drawn to Joseph, who, we are told, is quite handsome. Is Potiphar's wife physically attracted to Joseph because Potiphar has lost interest in her and is only concerned about the food on his plate?

If we didn't know what comes next, we might miss it. The passage only hints—and it's a very tiny hint—at the trouble that is to come. We will find in our continuing saga that plenty of trouble still awaits Joseph. But if God is with him, why the trouble? Well, who says that just because God is with him there will be no difficulties, no challenges or trials? If we were to insist that God's blessings mean we have no problems, then how do we account for Jesus' trial and persecution and death on a cross?

If Potiphar trusted Joseph, it appears that the secret to Joseph's success is that he trusted the Lord even more. Trust is not an easy commodity to come by. In fact, it runs counter to our human nature. It is simply in us to want to do things for ourselves and not become dependent on anyone else. But when we do learn to trust, we discover that trust does not stand by itself. It is supported and given nourishment and guidance by one's faith.

But then again, sometimes circumstances require that we put our trust in others. We have no other choice. That was certainly true of Joseph.

Dream Catcher

Barbara Brown Taylor tells of the time she was riding her horse on her farm in north Georgia. She attempted a jump between two trees, and the next thing she remembers is hearing the wail of the ambulance siren as she was being taken to the hospital. She doesn't know exactly what happened, but her guess is that one of those trees managed to get in her way. In the hospital, in addition to receiving several stitches to close the wound on her head, she was diagnosed with a severe concussion and was told to lie still, which she did for several days.

She describes the experience: having to use a bedpan because she had no balance with which to stand upright, enduring bizarre nightmares so vivid she fought to stay awake, not being able to think of certain words or finish sentences. "People took care of me," she says, "when I could not care for myself."

People like her—people like me (and you?)—don't like to be in that kind of situation. After all, as ministers, it is our nature to want to be of help to others, which means that in most cases we are not very good at receiving help from others when the need comes along. We prefer to be the helpers, not the helped.

Truth be told, you don't have to be a minister to resist wanting to have others take care of you, but it does seem to be particularly true of clergy types. Taylor admits this experience had a profound effect on her, and left her with the absolute need to depend on others. In telling about it, she refers to herself as a "damaged truster."[1]

We are all "damaged trusters," are we not? Well, so was Joseph.

When even our damaged trust overcomes our difficulties, and we find ourselves blessed by the Lord—whatever that blessing may be to us—others take notice, especially when those blessings are given to them as well. Referring first to Potiphar and then to Joseph, we are told that "His master saw that the LORD was with him . . . From the time that he made him overseer in his house and over all that he had, the LORD blessed the Egyptian's house for Joseph's sake" (Gen 39:4).

You see, trust begets trust. Blessings lead to more blessings. They are not always obvious, perhaps, but they are real.

1. Taylor, *Altar in the World*, 78–80.

The Blessing of the Lord

There are several considerations that come about through this portion of Joseph's life that have a direct impact on us. We need to think about what our blessings are, if for no other reason than they not only often come about through our difficulties but can be disguised as anything but blessings. We may need to re-define success, for it may come packaged in a way we don't recognize. We need to put our trust in Someone other than ourselves, even if we become damaged in the process. Damaged trust is still trust; maybe even the best kind.

If Joseph were with us today, offering his testimony of faith, my guess is that he would tell us, if he had the ability to change anything that happened to him he would choose not to do it. And since this is but the third installment in our consideration of Joseph's life, and if you know anything of his story at all, you are aware there is still plenty of drama and heartache and difficulties to come.

You see, trust and blessings go together. They do not necessarily make life easier, but they do go together. So put a bookmark on that word *trust*, if you will. It's going to continue to come in handy for our friend Joseph as he finds himself in even greater peril than what he has experienced already. And who knows, it might come in pretty handy for us as well.

Study/Thought Questions

1. Why do you think we are so deep into Joseph's story before God is mentioned?
2. Do you remember the age of seventeen? What are the characteristics that mark this age?
3. How do you picture Joseph's enslavement?
4. Put yourself in Joseph's sandals at this point in his life. How do you think you would have reacted to being sold into Potiphar's household?

5. What does the word *successful* mean to you? How would you define it in Joseph's case?

6. In Joseph's situation, how do success and trust go together? Consider that question in *your* life situation.

7. How good are you at trusting others when you consider yourself to be helpless? How good are you at trusting God?

8. Looking at your life journey, especially the difficulties you have endured, would you change anything? If so, what? If not, why?

The Lord Made It Prosper

*"Whatever was done there,
he was the one who did it"*

◈ GENESIS 39:22 ◈

WHEN it comes to faith, there are certain bedrock beliefs that rise above all other considerations, tenets that sustain when life seems to have become what can be a precarious journey. One of those for me is that, as a follower of Jesus, I cannot settle for merely believing the traditional doctrines that have been developed about him over the centuries. I must somehow make such beliefs personal, incorporating some into my behavior while discarding the others that simply don't seem to apply to who I am; or more importantly, to who I believe Jesus was. At the very heart of such a thought is that I must be, in my own personal way, the presence of Christ wherever I go.

Here's why it is so important: if you truly *are* the presence of Christ to others, there will be those occasions when it will be noticed—by someone. It won't happen every day, but on occasion a situation just may arise when you are with someone who takes notice of your behavior, your spirit and attitude. It's not a holy aura we're talking about, it's the sense that there is something about you that isn't about you. You have a presence, a purpose that goes beyond who you are. It is not something you provide or manufacture yourself. It is given as God's gift of grace to you, and then to the person you happen to be with at the time.

I don't know if you've ever thought of that before, but I do believe it to be true. And the reason I believe it is that Jesus himself said it would be so. You can look it up; you will find it in the Gospel of John (chapter 14).

The promise of God's presence, however, was not invented with the advent of the New Testament. It goes all the way back to the beginning of time, so you will also find it in the Book of Genesis. Take a look at Joseph's story, for example. Everything he touched, everything he did, had the Spirit of God about it. It was not something he created himself. The scriptures make it quite clear that all this came about through the blessing of Yahweh.

Not that it kept Joseph out of trouble, mind you.

In the preceding portion of the Joseph narrative (Gen 38), the one we considered in the previous chapter, we made note of Joseph's success. We are told that as he made his way in Potiphar's household, Joseph became successful; though, I will remind you, we suggested that the definition of success for Joseph might not mean the same as it generally does to us. In our discussion about this, we gave a great deal of emphasis to the word *trust*, and talked about how trust and faith go together. They certainly did for Joseph, and he became successful because of it.

That success spread to his master's house, and caught Potiphar's attention. "His master saw that the Lord was with Joseph," we are told, "and he became a successful man." So it did not take long for the captain of Pharaoh's guard to place his full confidence and trust in his young servant, which makes what happened next seem rather odd.

Today's story takes an abrupt and rather wicked turn, doesn't it? Because of that, we need to consider a different word in this portion of Joseph's unfolding story. While Joseph has become successful, and Potiphar has come to depend on Joseph for almost everything that happens in his household, Joseph remains quite vulnerable. That is the word to which we now give our attention in regard to this part of Joseph's life. Yes, things seem to be going along quite well, but Joseph finds himself to be *vulnerable*. That vulnerability is revealed through the enticements of Potiphar's wife.

Did you notice that we are not told her name? She simply remains "his master's wife." There's another side to this. When she lies and tells Potiphar that Joseph has attempted to take advantage of her, she doesn't refer to Joseph by name either. He is simply "the Hebrew." It is a way of diminishing the importance or personhood of the other. If you do not care for others or their behavior, you refer to them, not by their name but by their lineage or culture or ethnicity. And it is often done in a vulgar way. In this story, the writer does it when it comes to "the master's wife," and she does it by referring to Joseph as "the Hebrew."

In the eyes of the story writer she may just be Potiphar's wife, but that doesn't mean she has a minor role in this continuing saga. The chances are she's gotten used to getting her way. Her husband is an important man, and she has become accustomed to the trappings of a cushy life.

But sometimes that kind of life can be lonely and without purpose. If Potiphar has given over the running of the household to Joseph, so that he has no concern for anything other than the food he ate (39:6a), perhaps he has neglected his wife as well and not given her the attention she so obviously craves. If she is going to seek attention from another source, why not Joseph? After all, as the writer of this story puts it redundantly, Joseph "was handsome and good-looking" (Gen 39:6b).

Again, the word not used to describe Joseph, but which is obviously operative, is the word *vulnerable*. *Naive* might fit as well, for he should have been able to see that if "his master's wife" is so persistent in seeking his charms ("she spoke to Joseph day after day," we are told, and you can bet she's not discussing the weather), one day she will feel scorned by his continued rejections and turn on him. It is inevitable and it apparently doesn't take long.

Speaking of naive . . . Potiphar is obviously blind to what is going on in his own household. He has neglected his wife to the point that he can't see how she feels, nor does he evidently care.

But when, in her desperation, she concocts a vicious lie to get back at Joseph for his unwillingness to do her bidding, Potiphar immediately—did you notice it?—immediately takes her story for the truth. Without hesitation, he throws Joseph in the clinker.

There were plenty of gods in Egypt, some of whom may have garnered Potiphar's devotion. But because of the presence of Joseph in his household, he becomes aware of Joseph's God at least somewhat, and notes that "the Lord was with him" (Gen 39:3). If he has any sense of this, then he should have known that the story his wife has told him doesn't jive with what he has come to know about Joseph and his God. Yet, when push comes to shove, he accepts the word of his wife who tells him that Joseph has attempted to take sexual advantage of her. Evidently, Potiphar doesn't know Joseph very well, nor is he as aware of Joseph's God as we might think. Otherwise, he would have been suspicious of his wife, and not Joseph.

Once again, we are reassured that the Lord was with Joseph, even when he was put so abruptly behind bars. This time, the writer of this account goes beyond this rather simple promise of God's benevolence. He speaks of God's steadfast love toward Joseph.

The Hebrew word for this steadfast love is *hesed*, and is the Old Testament equivalent of the Greek word *agape*. It is selfless love, love that rises above one's own self-interest, and is used consistently in scripture as the kind of love that God shows toward God's human creation. And through this *hesed*, God favored Joseph in the sight of the jailer who was responsible for him during his incarceration.

Remember, at the beginning of this chapter how we talked about being the presence of Christ? Think of Joseph. Consider the pit in which he was thrown by his brothers, the rugged journey to Egypt and being sold as a slave to Potiphar. And though Joseph "found favor" in Potiphar's household and "attended him," becoming overseer of his house and "put in charge of all that he had"—meaning that he had a responsible position that afforded him some of the pleasures that Potiphar enjoyed—Joseph had to endure the daily, insistent overtures of Potiphar's possibly neglected

THE LORD MADE IT PROSPER

and definitely licentious wife. Now, after having become the victim of the resultant vulnerability, he finds himself in jail. It seems to be one tragedy after another when it comes to Joseph. He is either very up or he is very down. He just doesn't seem to be able to catch a break. With Joseph, it's either the high ground or the swamp. Nothing in his life appears to be consistent, or even fair.

The Bible is filled with fascinating stories such as this one. But I remind you, it is a book of faith, not a historical account of the life of Israel; at least, not in every case. If it were, it would provide us with more detail in narratives like this. For example, we aren't given a specific timeline for how long it takes all this to unfold. How long did Joseph work in Potiphar's household before his wife started applying pressure to Joseph? How long until she finally was given the opportunity to commit fraud against him? How long was it, after being jailed, that Joseph managed to gain the same level of trust with the jailer that he had done previously with Potiphar?

The kind of influence Joseph wielded, first with Potiphar and then the chief jailer, does not happen immediately. It takes time to develop relationships based on such trust. In Joseph's case, we can only guess. But we do have something to go on, enough information that the teller of Joseph's story keeps us intrigued. Allow me to explain . . .

We are told Joseph was in prison two years, and was thirty years of age when he was released into the administration of the Pharaoh. Remember that he was seventeen when we first meet him in scripture. That gives us some frame of reference, but only some. The way the story is told, that thirteen years goes by quickly, and those of us who are in the more wintry years of life can testify that this is how life is as it speeds right on by. Attempting to work all this out is part of the fun—yes, I said *fun*—of interpreting scripture. It requires that we add our own thoughts, or commentary, to these stories so we can bring them into our own experiences and make them real to us.

I have several sets of biblical commentaries accrued over my fifty-plus years of pastoral ministry. My first set was *The Broadman Bible Commentary,* produced through the Baptist Sunday

School Board publishing house in the late 60's. Then I purchased the original twelve-volume set of *The Interpreter's Bible*. When that post World War II commentary became dated, it was followed by the New *Interpreter's Bible*. I purchased that as well, and then the *Interpretation* series. My latest acquisition is *Feasting on the Word*, a set based on the lectionary readings. Almost all these volumes were purchased by subscription, one at a time. That's a lot of books and lot of financial investment.

You know what all that means? It means that the Bible is constantly being read line-by-line, and between the lines, by people smarter than I who are still trying to figure out, after all these centuries, what the Bible says. So they write about it and then sell it to clergy types like me.

I recall a conversation one Sunday with a physician and friend, an otolaryngologist. As we were about to enter the sanctuary for worship, we discussed how modern medicine does so well in diagnosing and treating illness, but that it does not always, in every case, get it right. "That's why we call it medical *practice*," he said to me.

Well, the same can be said of the Bible. We can't always know what the Bible means when it comes to its message. If we did, I wouldn't have had to buy all those sets of commentaries over the years. But then again, we wouldn't have much to talk about in church, either, as we journey together in trying to figure out what it means. Being the presence of Christ, recognizing that the Lord is with us and desires to be present to others through us, is not an exact way of life, to say the least. Nor is it easy. It takes time, it requires patience, and it calls for a constant devotion that finds us falling down and getting back up, falling down and getting back up.

So we don't know exactly how long it took for all the details of this portion of Joseph's life to unveil. We can only guess. But we do know that the last thing said of Joseph, before we go to the next adventure in his life, is that "because the Lord was with him, and whatever he did, the Lord made it prosper" (Gen 39:23). Just as we should not interpret the word *success*, in the context of Joseph's life, the same way we might in ours, the same can be said of *prosper*. How does one prosper in jail? Let's pursue that for a moment.

While in jail, Joseph manages to have a great deal of influence on the man who is in charge of his incarceration. As we will see in the next chapter, Joseph also comes into contact with those who have been in the household of Pharaoh. This means that slowly his influence is being seen and felt in the prison where he is kept. Joseph is doing more than just making do during this time of unfortunate circumstances. He is actually flourishing, prospering in this environment.

It is, of itself, a remarkable commentary on the kind of man he has become since we first were introduced to him. Everywhere he goes, with all the things that happen to him, Joseph makes the best of it, and goes even beyond that. He makes of it the kind of experience that shows to all those he encounters that the Lord is with him. Joseph is loyal to God because God is loyal to Joseph.

Can we say the same for ourselves?

Study/Thought Questions

1. What are your Christian beliefs?
2. Are such beliefs open to review, adaptation, change? If so, what criteria do you use?
3. What does being the presence of Christ mean to you?
4. How do you go about being the presence of Christ?
5. Why do you think Joseph was blessed by God in such a unique way?
6. Does trusting in God's mercy lead to vulnerability? If so, in what way(s)?
7. Do you view the Bible more as a historical account or a book of faith?

8. The author says, "Being the presence of Christ, recognizing that the Lord is with us and desires to be present to others through us, is not an exact way of life." Do you agree?

9. Is *loyalty* a theological concept? If so, how?

Dream Catcher

"Do not (dream) interpretations belong to God?"

GENESIS 40:8

IN the previous chapter we talked about how, because the Bible is a book of faith and not merely a historical account of the life of Israel, we are not given all the details of what happened in scriptural narratives. At least, not in every case. A perfect example is found in this part of Joseph's story. We are told that the Pharaoh's cupbearer and baker offended the king. Don't you want to know what they did to incur his wrath? I do.

Unfortunately, that's not a part of the biblical record. Evidently, the author of this story did not consider that detail to be important. However, having this information would make it more interesting, don't you think? After all, the baker eventually lost his life over it. What was it they had done that called for imprisonment? Were they dipping in the till? Were they attempting a coup, colluding together or with others? Or was it as simple as being in the wrong place at the wrong time? What was going on?

We aren't told. We just know they got thrown in the hoosegow, as did Joseph. Evidently, in Egypt it doesn't take much, when you are close to the edges of power—or as Walter Brueggemann refers to it, "the ways of the empire"[1]—to get into trouble. That's

1. Brueggemann/Mays, *Interpretation: Genesis*, 320.

what happened with Joseph when his master's wife turned on him after he spurned her amorous advances. You know what can take place when you play with fire. Well, the same can be said of power. Sometimes you get burned, and at this point in Joseph's life you can mark him pretty much well done—or at least charred.

Another point we made previously is that in these narratives we aren't given specific time-lines for how long it took the drama to unfold. It happens again here in this portion of the story. While incarcerated, Joseph is put in charge of the Pharaoh's servants, the ones who had been imprisoned for whatever they had done to offend the king. And according to the way it is told, "they continued for some time in custody" (Gen 40:4). Okay. "Some time." It's the best we have, so we'll just have to accept it.

But that doesn't keep us from guessing, does it? A few months? Possibly. We do know Joseph was imprisoned two years, so it was certainly within that time frame. But two years can seem like more than just "some time." When you are behind bars it can feel, I would think, like an eternity.

Regardless, one night both the cupbearer and the baker have dreams. What they don't know is that they are in the presence of the dream catcher, one who has been interpreting dreams from an early age. Now that he's pushing thirty, Joseph has gotten really good at it. As we know, it got him in trouble when he was unable to keep from using his dreams as the means to lord it over his brothers. Now, he puts his God-given abilities to a better, more productive, use.

Evidently, Joseph also has the gift of discernment; not that it takes a genius to figure out when someone is having a bad day. "Why are your faces downcast today?" he asks them. "We have had dreams," they reply, "and there is no one to interpret them" (Gen 40:7–8).

Let's pause for just a moment so I can ask you a question. Do you have dreams? Sure, we all do. Do you become despondent when you can't interpret what your dreams mean? I doubt it. Chances are, we just pass them off as meaningless and don't attempt to attach any specific significance to them. But, when we are going through stress, which can be both negative or positive depending on the circumstances, dreams operate on a wholly different level. They may just be our subconscious telling us something about what is truly important. It is good, especially in those times, to listen to what our dreams tell us.

That is what Pharaoh's servants are attempting to do. "We have had dreams, and there is no one to interpret them." And Joseph responds, "Do not interpretations belong to God?" (Gen 40:8). I find that to be an interesting response. Do you? Let's dissect it and see what it says to us.

First of all, it is doubtful that when Joseph mentions God his two fellow prisoners know to whom he is referring. Since Joseph is a Hebrew, he is thinking of Yahweh, the God of his fathers Abraham, Isaac, and Jacob. And even that concept of God was fairly primitive compared to an ever-evolving theological understanding that will continue to unfold in scripture, especially in regard to God's unique relationship with the Hebrews. At this point, Joseph's cell mates probably consider Joseph's God in generic terms, with a small *g*. So it is quite possible that when Joseph mentions God, the cupbearer and baker might have wondered which god he is talking about. After all, in Egypt there are many gods.

It could be, I suppose, that the Egyptians had some indication of the kind of God the Hebrews worshiped. But remember: this is long before Moses. Moses came on the scene at a time in Egypt's life when "a new king arose over Egypt, who did not know Joseph" (Exod 1:8). Some forty years later, when God calls to Moses from the burning bush, Moses himself seems to be unaware of the Hebrew God, or who God is. So by the time of the exodus, due to four centuries of slavery, Israel has lost touch with their God and has to be introduced to Yahweh all over again. And even then, God refers to God's self in what could be considered fairly vague terms. "I AM WHO I AM," God says to Moses. "Tell them I AM has sent you" (Exod 3:14).

But during the time of Joseph, when he shares cell space with the servants of Pharaoh, he is keenly aware of his God, even in a land of many gods where there is a god for this, a god for that.

These two men, the cupbearer and the baker, may very well have been confused when Joseph refers only to God and is not specific about which god it is. Does Joseph mean the god who is responsible for dreams? No, Joseph means the God who is responsible for *everything*.

Another point: Joseph doesn't take credit for his ability to interpret their dreams, or any other dreams, for that matter. All interpretations, he says, belong to God. This attitude may very well go back to a point we have made before, namely that God's blessings on Joseph are not something Joseph has earned. Like grace, God has chosen to bestow these blessings on Joseph, and seems to be willing to place them in his hands as a worthy steward of this grace. What Joseph does with those blessings is key to his story. He makes the best of them, and in gratitude gives God all the credit. "Do not interpretations belong to God?" It may very well be Joseph's way of letting them know, or possibly acknowledging to God, that *everything* belongs to God.

While the cupbearer and the baker might not necessarily agree with Joseph's theology, they're not in a position to quibble. As they say, beggars can't be choosers. They will listen to anyone who seems to have the answers they are seeking.

It is at this point that the teller of Joseph's story does become specific about time. The cupbearer's dream has to do with grapes; three branches of ripened grapes, in fact. They yield their fruit, Pharaoh's servant presses them in his master's cup, and places it in his hand. And Joseph says to him, "Easy peasy. The three branches represent the three days in which Pharaoh will bring you out of jail and back into service."

And then Joseph asks a favor. When the cupbearer stands again before Pharaoh, would he put in a good word for him? Joseph has done well in prison. In fact, you may recall that we are told he prospers. But jail is still jail. Will the cupbearer mention him to Pharaoh and ask him to "get me out of this place"? "I was stolen out of the land of the Hebrews," he explains, "and here also I have done nothing that they should have put me into the dungeon" (Gen 40:15).

Oh, now it's a dungeon, not just a prison. Big difference, I would think. By helping the Pharaoh's servants, Joseph sees a bit of light at the end of the dungeon, and he uses this as an opportunity to plead his case in the highest court in the land. Unfortunately, as we will see, once the cupbearer is given his freedom, despite Joseph's request, he completely forgets about seeing to the freedom of the dream catcher. With some people, gratitude is short-lived if not short-sighted.

And then there is the baker. His news is not so good. He figures that if the cupbearer is going to be freed, surely his news will be equally positive. Not so, unfortunately. Why he would incur the Pharaoh's cruel wrath, again we do not know. But, not surprisingly, his dream has to do with his vocation, just as it had with the cupbearer. And again the number is three, in this case three baskets of baked goods placed on top of his head, from which birds are eating, taking their fill.

Joseph's interpretation is as easy to come by as the first, but not so easy to tell. Nevertheless, since the baker asked for the meaning behind his dream, Joseph gives it to him, apparently without hesitation. The three baskets, like the grape branches, represent three days. But in his case, it means that in three days he will lose his head, and then it will be hung on a pole and the birds will eat the man's flesh.

It all comes true. On the third day, the cupbearer is restored to Pharaoh's service and the baker loses his life, which just happens to be Pharaoh's birthday. You would think, unless it was his fortieth birthday, that he would be in a magnanimous mood. But not necessarily. Pharaoh did sponsor a feast for his servants to mark his special day. The entertainment was the restoration of the cupbearer to the king's good graces and the unfortunate execution of the baker, proving that cruelty knows no season or occasion.

Obviously, this portion of Joseph's story is not really about the two men with whom he shares jail space. It is about Joseph, and how these encounters continue his unfolding journey from the land of his father Jacob to the home of Potiphar, the captain of the king's guard, and finally into the service of Pharaoh himself where eventually he will be reunited with his family.

But there is a sense in which the lesson to be learned from this story isn't finally and ultimately about Joseph either. Look at this from the viewpoint of a panorama. If Joseph had not been taken into Egypt, the chances are that his people, the Hebrews, would have been decimated by the eventual seven-year famine. True, the Jews would not have had to suffer all those years of slavery, but if there had been no slavery there would have been no need for an exodus. The exodus was responsible for the formation of the Hebrews as a nation of twelve tribes. Otherwise, they might have been, at best, a loosely-connected group of kindred without any real sense of nationality. If that had been the case, the entire history of Israel would have been completely changed, if there would have been an Israel in existence at all. And the God who called them to be a special, set-apart people might very well have been forgotten.

What does that say to you? Is there a lesson here? I think so. It says to me that what we do right now, the decisions we make in the moment, have repercussions for all that is to happen from now on. When we dream, the chances are our dreams are a semi-conscious projection of what has already happened to us. In the biblical literature we refer to as the Old Testament, dreams are more about the future than they are the past, a future that is shaped by what is done right now.

As we have mentioned before, one of the more interesting elements in Joseph's unfolding saga is that there is little mention of God. Yes, Joseph does give God credit for the interpretations of dreams. Otherwise, God seems to be in the background observing what is going on, ready at any moment to turn these events toward God's eventual purpose. Or, as Barbara Brown Taylor puts it, "Sometimes the work of God's hands is so evident that you can see it a mile away and sometimes you have to dust for fingerprints."[2]

How do we see the work of God's hands in the life of Joseph? The same way we see it in our own lives: we open our eyes to what

---

2. Taylor, *Gospel Medicine*, 120.

is going on around us, and as we respond to life we place ourselves in the hands of the One who will gently guide us toward God's light.

I remind you, there will come a time when a king arises in Egypt who will not know Joseph. Until Joseph's story is told centuries later by the chroniclers of Israel, his memory will have faded into the sunset that presides over the sands of Egypt. But who remembers the name of the Pharaoh who knew not Joseph? You see, it just goes to show that power is not in Pharaoh's hands, or in the hands of any human leader (a good lesson to learn, especially during any election season), but in God's.

It may take a long while, but God does not forget God's people. God has an eternal plan. You may wonder what it is and what place you have in it all, but do believe that God's eyes are on you, to guide you in such a way that your life has meaning in the kingdom of heaven. What you decide to do with your life, right now, will shape what is to come for you and for those around you. Or, as Peter Marty puts it, "To enjoy the miracle of now is to appreciate the confidence God has in us for crafting a future."[3]

May you find yourself confidently in the hands of the One who has a purpose for you, and may all your dreams come true.

Study/Thought Questions

1. The author notes that when it comes to scripture, primarily narratives, we are often not given all the details. What "gaps" in scripture do you wish were filled? How do you fill them for yourself?

2. The Hebrew scholar Walter Brueggemann is cited as referring to "the ways of the empire." What does that mean to you? How does it apply today?

3. What is the gift of discernment?

---

3. Marty, *Christian Century*, October 26, 2016, 3.

4. The author says that dreams may be our subconscious telling us something about what is truly important. What do your dreams tell you?
5. Do you consider yourself a steward of God's grace?
6. How do your dreams speak of the future?
7. Peter Marty says, "To enjoy the miracle of now is to appreciate the confidence God has in us for crafting a future." Do you agree? If so, what are you doing about it?

Plenty and Want

"All the world came to Joseph in Egypt"

GENESIS 41:57

Another two years have passed since Joseph correctly interpreted the dreams of the cupbearer and the baker, and Joseph continues to languish in jail. Though the word *languish* is not used in the *New Revised Standard Version*, my translation choice generally, I think it accurately describes how Joseph must have been feeling at this time in his life.

So I looked up the word *languish*. It means "waste," "yearn," "ache." If we had to choose one of those three, in Joseph's case perhaps the word *ache* is a more appropriate expression for how he must feel. He aches for the freedom he once enjoyed, a longing made even more poignant by his knowing that he has done nothing wrong for him to be cast into jail in the first place.

Earlier, we are told he prospers in jail. The two words, prosper and languish, don't seem to go together, do they? But I think, in this case, the word *prosper* has a unique meaning. Perhaps it means that Joseph does as well as he can, given his situation, and makes the best of his circumstances, a dynamic that will prove to serve him well for the future. That would still leave some room for languishing, don't you think?

But things are about to turn for the dream catcher, for the better. This time it is Pharaoh who dreams. He is standing on the banks of the Nile and observes as seven sleek and fat cows emerge from the water and begin to graze on the reed grass. Then, seven ugly and thin cows come from the river. They do not eat of the grass but simply stand by the other, healthier cows, then commence to eating them.

That's it. Not a long dream, but surely a vivid one; at least graphic enough that it wakes him up. He goes back to sleep only to have another dream. This dream also involves the number seven, except this time it is not cows but ears of grain. The first seven are plump and good, all growing on one stalk. They are followed by seven more ears, thin and blighted and not edible at all. However, the thin ears ravenously swallow up the plump ears, and once again Pharaoh awakes. This time, he does not go back to sleep.

And he is irritable. His spirit is troubled, we are told, so he sends for his magicians and wise men. Pharaoh needs—actually, Pharaoh demands—an explanation for these strange dreams, and whenever Pharaoh demands something Pharaoh expects an answer. He's out of luck, however, because none of his confidants, despite their best efforts, can tell him the meaning of his dreams.

And that's when Pharaoh's cupbearer remembers Joseph's request, made while they were in prison together. "Remember me when it is well with you," Joseph had asked him. "Please do me the kindness to make mention of me to Pharaoh, and so to get me out of this place" (Gen 40:14).

"I remember my faults today," (Gen 41:9) the cupbearer says to his king, which is another way of saying, "Uh oh, now I remember. There is a young Hebrew . . . " He tells the king about Joseph, and Pharaoh, desperate enough to seek help even from a Hebrew, sends for him.

We have talked about how these stories of Joseph don't often have the details we would like, and because of it we have to read somewhat between the lines. It is the way of scripture. We also know, because of physics, that for every action there is an equal and opposite reaction, and that is true in this case. Just when we are not provided what we think would be helpful details, we are given that which seems not to be necessary at all. For example, we are told that Joseph shaved himself and changed his clothes. Well, yeah, who wouldn't?

The only reason I can think this is important for us to know is that Joseph recognizes the importance of having an audience with Pharaoh. And let's face it: prison dungeons don't exactly call for the best in personal hygiene. But it may go beyond that. He also is aware that this may be his chance, his only chance, to get out of the prison that has housed him these last few years, and he's going to make the best of it. He wants to look as presentable as possible to the king, so he spruces up a bit.

Still, what purpose does it serve to the story? After all, we are given no indication that Pharaoh notices Joseph's appearance. He has other things on his mind and immediately gets to the point. "I have had a dream . . . I have heard it said of you that when you hear a dream you can interpret it."

"Oh yes," Joseph says to the king. "Lay it on me. I can do it. I am really good at this sort of thing." No, once again Joseph gives all the credit to his God. "God will give Pharaoh a favorable answer," he tells the king (Gen 41:16). Say this about Joseph, he is consistent in giving all the glory to God. He has done it before and now he does it again.

Let's pause for a moment and review just a bit.

How long was Joseph in the pit back in Dothan? We don't know, but any time was too long. How long was he in the service of Potiphar, the captain of Pharaoh's guard? We aren't told, but he had to endure the enticements of Potiphar's wife just about the entire time. How long was he in jail? Ah, that we are told. It has been more than two years since Joseph has seen the light of day. That means he is now at least thirty years of age. If so, it has been thirteen years since his brothers sold him to the Ishmaelites, who in turn sold Joseph to Potiphar. And in all that time Joseph has never forgotten his God. He may have uttered a few "poor me's" along the way, but when push comes to shove, he gives all the glory to God. We dare not forget that, not if we want to understand Joseph's story.

Speaking of Joseph's story, let's go back to our current narrative. Pharaoh repeats his dreams of the cows and the ears of grain, and Joseph tells him the two dreams are one and the same. Perhaps the king has had two dreams lest he decides the first one holds little or no importance.

We made the point in the previous chapter that in the Old Testament, especially, dreams have less to do with what has happened in the past than they do with foretelling the future. That is true in this case. Joseph informs Pharaoh there will be seven years of plenty followed by seven years of want, or famine. The fact that Pharaoh has had two dreams means that this is a done deal of which there is no question. It is "fixed by God," Joseph says, "and God will shortly bring it about" (Gen 41:32).

If Pharaoh's confidants cannot interpret his dreams, it stands to reason they can't help him figure out a solution for all of this either. But Joseph, the dream catcher, can. He provides the king with a plan for storing grain during the first seven good years, so they can have it available in reserve for the next seven bad years.

Pharaoh is considered as more than just a king in Egypt. He is a god, and there is no reason to think that he has not bought into that way of thinking, that he does not look at himself as divine. But even Pharaoh, lord of the greatest nation on earth, one who commands the mightiest army and has servants to do his every bidding, stands no chance in the face of famine. So he is willing to give the young Hebrew the opportunity to provide the answers he is seeking.

It's a win-win situation when you think about it. Look at it from the Pharaoh's perspective. If Joseph is correct in his dream interpretation, the people will be saved. If he is not, Egypt will still have grain stored away for their use, and he will simply do to Joseph what he did to the baker: off with his head.

Except, Pharaoh doesn't appear to be hedging his bets. He seems to have full faith in Joseph and his abilities. So Joseph's plan pleases Pharaoh. Even more, Pharaoh seems to have a fairly clear understanding of Joseph's God, who he recognizes as the architect of all this. "Since God has shown you all this, there is no one so discerning and wise as you. You shall be over my house..." (Gen 41:40).

Sounds familiar, doesn't it? Deja vu all over again! Whenever Joseph has the opportunity to show his worth, he is rewarded for it, whether it is in the house of Potiphar, the captain of Pharaoh's guard, or the house of Pharaoh himself. The king gives Joseph control of his house, he takes his signet ring off his finger and gives it to Joseph, provides him an unlimited credit account at Neiman Marcus, invites him to ride shotgun in his own personal chariot, and places him second in command over all of Egypt.

But he's not through. Look what's behind door number two! Pharaoh changes Joseph's name, evidently a great honor in that part of the world. It would mean that Joseph is now officially an Egyptian. It has been decreed, by Pharaoh no less. From now on, in Egypt Joseph will be known as Zaphenath-paneah. It isn't as simple as *Joseph*, but it does have a certain ring to it. Zaphenath-paneah. However, if it's all right with you, we'll stick to *Joseph*, if for no other reason than it's a bit easier to pronounce. Oh, and Pharaoh gives him a wife, Asenath the daughter of Potiphera, the priest of On.

Talk about going from the dungeon to the penthouse—literally! But Joseph evidently doesn't let it go to his head. Maybe that's because he doesn't have the time. Joseph, aka Zaphenath-paneah, has a job to do. He rides Pharaoh's chariot all over Egypt for seven years, gathering up food while there is still plenty to gather up. He stores it in the cities, putting it under lock and key. There is so much grain it looks like the grains of sand beside the sea. Finally, he stops measuring the grain because, as we are told, "it was beyond measure" (Gen 41:49).

During this time Joseph and his wife Asenath have two sons. You might think, since he is now officially Egyptian, he would give them Egyptian names out of gratitude for Pharaoh's kindness, not to mention that he is married to a daughter of Egypt. But no, in keeping with his consistent faith in God he gives his first son the Hebrew name Manasseh, for "God has made me forget all my hardship and all my father's house." His second son he names

Ephraim, "For God has made me fruitful in the land of my misfortunes" (Gen 41:52).

How about a re-review? Think of all the difficulties Joseph has endured: thrown into a pit by his angry and murderous brothers, sold into slavery, brought to Egypt where he is a servant to Potiphar, and dumped into jail because he refuses the enticements of his master's wife. Still, after all is said and done, he recognizes that everything that has happened to him has been for a purpose, God's purpose. "God has made me fruitful in the land of my misfortunes."

Egypt, of course, did indeed experience seven years of want after enjoying seven years of plenty. And it wasn't just Egypt. All the surrounding nations suffered from the famine. Not Egypt, however. Joseph opened the storehouses and provided the people with enough grain to see them through. And "all the world came to Joseph in Egypt to buy grain," we are told. "All the world came to Joseph" (Gen 41:57).

The dream catcher is now experiencing a dream of his own.

I wonder what went through Joseph's mind and heart during those two plus years he was in prison. We know of the dream interpretations of Pharaoh's cupbearer and baker, dreams which came true within three days. We are aware that the chief jailer gave Joseph the responsibility of basically overseeing the prison and its activities. But we are told nothing else. Why do you think that is?

Maybe it is because nothing else of any importance happened. And all the while Joseph waited, perhaps wondering himself if the cupbearer remembered him to Pharaoh. Do you recall that when Joseph received the message that he was to appear before the king the first thing he did was shave and change his clothes? Can't you just see him standing in front of the mirror saying, "The cupbearer did remember me. The cupbearer did remember me." After two whole years! Except, knowing Joseph as we do, the chances are much higher that he said, "The Lord has remembered me! The Lord has remembered me!" The promise of God has come through.

When you think about it, that is what the holy scriptures are all about, revealing to us through the stories of humans like

Pharaoh and Joseph, like Abraham and Jacob, like the prophets and finally Jesus, that all God's promises do indeed come true.

A man named Everet R. Storms read the Bible through twenty-seven times. It was during his final reading of the Bible that Storms wrote down all the promises found in scripture. He counted 8,810 promises. Of those, he figured that 7,487 were made by God to his human creation.[1]

I'm certainly in no position to quibble about this. I've spent my lifetime studying scripture, but can't say I've read it through that many times. So I will take Brother Storms at his word. But I can say this: a lot of my life, and my guess is that it's true of you as well, has been spent, like Joseph, waiting. What have you been waiting for? The diagnosis, perhaps, or possibly waiting for your loved one's diagnosis . . . waiting for your job to get better, your children to do well, your life to improve, your ship to come in . . . waiting, waiting.

Joseph waited for the cupbearer to honor his word. It took two years, but finally he did. But again, it is not the cupbearer who deserves the credit here. It is God, who, as the prophet Isaiah centuries later says to the people of Israel, "I have inscribed you on the palms of my hands" (Isa 49:16).

So if you find yourself waiting—for whatever it may be—do it in faithfulness, trusting that God has your name inscribed, not only on the palm of God's hand, but in the very depths of God's heart. And know that when life gives you plenty, or you find yourself in want, God will see you through.

That's a promise.

Study/Thought Questions

1. What does the word *languish* mean to you? Have you ever experienced this?
2. What does the word *prosper* mean to you? Can *languish* and *prosper* go together?

---

1. Swindoll and Hough, *Pit to Pinnacle*, 28

3. The pharaoh changes Joseph's name, giving him an Egyptian moniker. Do you think that is important to the story? If so, why?

4. Joseph gives his sons Hebrew names. What do you think is the significance of this?

5. Joseph's testimony is that "God has made me fruitful in the land of my misfortunes." Does that apply to your life experience? If so, how?

6. What promise(s) are you waiting for?

BROTHERS

"Joseph's brothers came and bowed themselves before him"

GENESIS 42:6

IN 1939, John Steinbeck published his classic novel, *Grapes of Wrath*. The story depicts the struggles of people from Oklahoma—*Okies*, they were called—escaping the drought conditions of the Dust Bowl. It may have been a novel, but it was based on real life. Tens of thousands of people abandoned their farms when the winds blew away the topsoil in which they had been growing their crops. Many of them, as Steinbeck describes it, made their way to California, seeking a better life.

Perhaps it was not unlike the famine experienced in Joseph's day, not only in Egypt but throughout what we now call the Middle East. People came from all over to buy grain in Egypt, for it seems the Egyptians were the only ones who could see it coming and were prepared for it. Of course, they were prepared because of Joseph's ability to interpret Pharaoh's dreams and then act upon it.

Like a movie director who shifts from one scene in a certain locale to another, the writer of Joseph's story does the same. In this new, unfolding scene, up close we see the grizzled, bearded, sandstone face of an old man. His name is Jacob and he lives in the land of Canaan. He emerges from the dwelling he calls his home, and squints his eyes. Once he adjusts to the glare of the morning sun,

Jacob sees his sons standing around whispering to one another. They are not working, as they should be, they are speaking to one another in low, hushed tones.

It is obvious to the old man that they don't want him to hear their conversation, but Jacob will have none of that. If they've got something to say, especially about him, let them say it to his face. "Why do you keep looking at one another?" (Gen 42:1) he says to them, which may just be his way of saying, "Okay, boys, spill the beans. You've got something on your mind? Let's hear it."

Or, it could be that because of the drought they've got nothing else to do but stand around looking at each other. The herds are decimated, the ground so hard they cannot grow crops. If they were to go to work, just exactly what is it they would do? Well, Jacob will give them something to do. "I've heard there is grain in Egypt. Go down and buy some of it before we starve to death" (Gen 42:2). So they did. But Benjamin, the youngest of Jacob's twelve sons, did not go.

We don't know how old Benjamin is by now—at least in his mid-twenties, I would think—but do you remember the affection Jacob had for Joseph because he was the son of Jacob's beloved Rachel? Well, Jacob feels the same toward Benjamin. He's lost one of Rachel's sons, he's not going to take a chance on losing the other. Benjamin is of double value to Jacob, not only because he was the son of Rachel, but because she died while bringing him into the world. Has Jacob spoiled Benjamin as he so obviously did Joseph? We don't know.[1] What we are aware of is that Jacob will do nothing to jeopardize the life of his youngest son. Egypt may have plenty of grain, but it's got cutthroats, thieves and murderers too. Who knows what might happen over there. No, he's not going to risk it.

When we lived in northeast Arkansas, my wife Janet worked as a long-term substitute teacher. One spring the school planned a field trip for her class. They were going to Little Rock to visit the capitol. One of the mothers wouldn't let her child participate.

---

1. For an odd twist to the relationship between Jacob and his youngest son Benjamin, see Gen 50:27.

BROTHERS

There were gangs in Little Rock, she told Janet. It was just too dangerous. When told of her objections, my response was that yes indeed there were gang members at the capitol; and they all wore suits and were referred to as legislators!

Jacob's ten oldest sons can handle themselves in a foreign country like Egypt, but he isn't about to risk danger coming to his youngest child Benjamin, the son of Rachel. He might encounter legislators! They do not argue with papa. They gather their belongings, take the money from Jacob's hand to be used to purchase grain, and make their way to Egypt land. They will have to get in line, however. The closer they get to Egypt, the more they realize that people have come from all over that part of the world to buy grain.

I've noticed a trend in retail sales these days. Perhaps you have too. When you walk into the store—whether it's home goods, hardware or hamburgers—the employee nearest you calls out loudly, "Welcome to the Widget Store (or whatever they sell). How may we assist you?" Not help, assist. Except, that is, for my recent venture to the drug store. When I came through the entrance, the young lady behind the register, who had obviously been trained to greet incoming customers, said in a low, mumbling, quite insincere voice, "Welcome to Walgreens." It made me feel so warm all over (note the sarcasm).

That's *not* exactly how they operated in Egypt during the famine. They didn't even mumble a greeting. In fact, the only thing that greeted the ten sons of Jacob was suspicion. Of course, what they don't know is that they are standing before their very own brother, identified to them as the Egyptian governor. They aren't standing very long, however. In true Middle Eastern fashion, and because they are more like beggars than buyers, they bow prostrate at Joseph's feet.

This is where the story truly becomes fascinating. Immediately, Joseph knows who they are. They don't recognize him, however. Remember, he was seventeen when they threw him in that pit. He is now pushing forty, and has obviously changed in appearance, and their lack of awareness gives Joseph the upper hand.

"Where do you come from?" he asks harshly.
"From the land of Canaan. We've come to buy food."

And for some reason, the writer of this account repeats himself, telling us that Joseph recognizes his brothers but they don't know who he is. Maybe he feels he didn't get the idea over strongly enough the first time. So let's be clear: Joseph knows who they are, but they don't have a clue as to his identity. Got it? Good.

Joseph also remembers the dreams he had when he was still a teenager, the ones that made his brothers so angry they threw him into a pit and sold him into slavery. And speaking of repeating ourselves . . . I will remind you of a point we have already made more than once, that in that place and time dreams had less to do with what had already happened than with foretelling what was yet to come.

In one dream, the sons of Jacob were binding sheaves of wheat in the field. Joseph's sheaf rose and stood upright, while the other sheaves, representing his brothers, bowed down at its feet. In another dream, the sun, the moon, and eleven stars (again, obviously his brothers) were bowing down to him. That one even got Jacob's dander up, because now he is also one of those bowing before Joseph. Joseph was his favorite son, and Jacob made no bones about it. But he didn't take kindly to the idea that the whole family was to bow down to his son, even if he was the offspring of Rachel.

Now, more than twenty years later, the memory of it is rolling like a stampede of horses down Joseph's mind when he spies his brothers bowing before him, just as his dreams had once foretold. Imagine!

What was Joseph's motivation for what comes next? Apparently, it is quite simple. He notices that Benjamin is not with them, and he desperately aches to see his little brother. He can't return to Canaan with them, he has a life here in Egypt—a wife and two sons, a responsible position. He is the governor over all the land, after all, made even more responsible because of the severe drought they are experiencing. There is only one thing to do: Benjamin must come to him. But how? Quickly, Joseph concocts a plot. "You are spies!" he says to his brothers. "You are spies! You have come to see the nakedness of the land!"

His brothers object, but nothing they say can seemingly change his mind. They try to explain who they are. There had been twelve of them, they tell Joseph. One of the twelve, the youngest, has stayed with their father. The other has been lost "and is no more" (Gen 42:13).

Then this is what they will do. One of the brothers is to return to Canaan, but he dare not return to Egypt unless he brings the youngest son back with him. It will prove their story, Joseph says to them, and if it isn't true they will experience the wrath of Pharaoh. And then, to give them a little taste of their own medicine, he throws them into jail for three days where they can think long and hard about what he has said to them.

The brothers may not recognize Joseph, but surely they know he is a Hebrew and not Egyptian. You and I might not be able to tell the difference, but they certainly could. And Joseph admits to them that he fears Yahweh, the God of the Jews, so at least they are becoming aware that their lives may not be in danger.

After three days, Joseph comes to see them in the prison. This time, he reverses himself. Instead of sending one of the brothers back home to fetch Benjamin, he decides to send nine, leaving one of them to remain in Egypt in jail. But the end goal is the same. Upon their return, they are to bring Benjamin with them.

Like the statute of limitations when it comes to murder, guilt remains forever. Immediately, the brothers associate this situation with what they had done more than twenty years before in Dothan. "Alas, we are paying the penalty for what we did to our brother. His anguish is now our anguish." And Reuben, the eldest son of Jacob, tells his younger brothers, "I told you so. I told you not to hurt Joseph. But you wouldn't listen. You had murder in your eyes and vengeance in your heart. After all these years, there is now a reckoning for Joseph's blood" (Gen 42:22).

And all the while, Joseph is standing there listening to every word. He has been speaking the Egyptian language to them through an interpreter so as not to give away his identity. The

53

brothers do not know he can understand what they are saying. Imagine, if you will, the feelings of regret, of misunderstanding, the intensity and emotion that fill that prison cell—on both sides. But instead of feeling a sense of revenge, or even justice, for finally getting even with his brothers for what they did to him, Joseph feels a deep, deep sadness; perhaps for all the years that have been lost to him and to his family. He turns away from his brothers so they cannot see him weeping.

Of the ten brothers, why Joseph picked Simeon to remain we do not know. Perhaps—and this is strictly conjecture on my part—it was Simeon who had been particularly cruel to Joseph when he had been thrown into the pit. Handcuffing Simeon in front of the others, Joseph loaded them down with grain and sent them back to their father.

When Jacob's sons returned and told him their story, they explained to their father what the Egyptian governor had demanded. Then they began opening the bags of grain. In them they found their money, the funds from which they were to have paid for the grain. Something strange is going on here, but no one can understand what it is, nor why. Up to this point, Jacob has said nothing in response to what they have told him; now he does. Essentially he says to his sons, "This is all your fault. Because of you I have lost Joseph, now Simeon, and now you want me to lose Benjamin too?"

Remember when Reuben intervened with his brothers in Dothan the day they wanted to kill Joseph? He told them to spare his life, there would be no bloodshed (Gen 37:22). It is now time for Reuben to rise to the occasion again, and he does so in a drastic measure. "If I don't bring Benjamin back to you, you may kill my two sons. I take full responsibility for what happens."

Regardless of how you may feel about that, understand that we are considering this ancient Middle Eastern story from twenty-first century mind-sets. How in the world could the sacrifice of Reuben's sons make up for the loss of Joseph, and the potential loss of Simeon and Benjamin? Perhaps Reuben was simply using this as a way of taking upon himself the responsibility of his little brother. Maybe he was, if you will excuse the pun, *dead* serious. Or it could be he anticipated Jacob's response.

We are informed that old stubborn Jacob refuses to send Benjamin to Egypt with his brothers. But eventually, they run out of the grain they had retrieved and brought home. They will have no choice but to return. We are not told how long the grain lasted, but we can be assured that all the while Simeon is cooling his heels back in an Egyptian prison. We can also suspect that Joseph's mind is filled with thoughts of his father's home. Did his brothers convey his message? How did Jacob respond? How long would it take for them to return to Egypt? What is happening?

But there may be a larger question involved, certainly on the mind of the narrative's author. What is God's plan in all this? Joseph's motive for his subterfuge is that he might be reunited with his brother Benjamin. But there's another layer to this encounter. We can't help but think that he sees the surprising visit of his brothers as God's means of bringing the family back together. Joseph could have immediately identified himself to his brothers, but if he had it would have placed the impending results in their hands. Joseph wants to put it in God's hands instead.

Are we willing to do the same?

The political life of our nation these last few years has been quite revealing as to where we are and what kind of people we are. Many are delighted at what has transpired, others are not. I don't think it can be argued that we are a divided country in our sentiments. The question is, how should we, as followers of Jesus, respond? May I offer this . . .

On that fateful day when the sons of Jacob bowed down before their brother Joseph, just as his dreams had foretold, none of them knew what would happen as a result of this unlikely reunion. Neither did Joseph, of course. And while Joseph did indeed use some trickery to bring it about, it is still quite clear that he left the results up to God.

I suggest we do the same, which doesn't mean we can or should do nothing. We still have much work to do, the least of which is to vote and to vote our conscience. Consider what Joseph did. In our efforts to seek justice for all people, to speak and live kindly, to walk humbly with our God, we are challenged to do it now in new and more intense ways.

It could be argued that we have no other choice, but in truth we do. Hold dearly to your faith, trust in the God we serve, and believe that in God's eternal wisdom all we do, and the manner in which we respond, will be of witness to the presence of the kingdom of heaven in our midst.

Is that the choice you will make? Well, is it?

Study/Thought Questions

1. The author likens this portion of Joseph's story to a movie. If you were the director, how would you frame the scene of Jacob and his sons?
2. The author of this biblical account tells us twice that Joseph recognized his brothers while they did not know him. Why the redundancy?
3. How do you think Joseph might have felt hearing his brothers describe him as the one who "was lost and is no more"?
4. Why do you think Joseph cast his brothers into jail for three days? Is he being vengeful?
5. After those three days, why did Joseph change his strategy?
6. Why do you think Joseph picked Simeon to remain in Egypt?
7. The author cites the big question in this portion of the narrative: what is God's plan in all this? What do you think it is?
8. The author ties Joseph's narrative to today's political climate. Do you agree? If so, where do you see parallels?
9. Discuss the "odd twist" the author refers to in regard to the relationship between Jacob and his youngest son Benjamin. How do you see this unfolding?

The Baby of the Family

"Then he looked up and saw his brother Benjamin"

GENESIS 43:29

THE sons of Jacob, grain in hand, have returned from Egypt to the land of their father. That part of the world has been hit with a severe famine, and because of the judicious foresight of the Egyptians—namely, Joseph the governor of Egypt—people from all over have come to purchase grain so they might not starve. The family of Jacob is no different.

Unbeknownst to them, Jacob's sons have met with their brother Joseph, the one they had, years earlier, sold into slavery. If they can tell, as I suspect, that the governor is Hebrew and not Egyptian, the author makes no mention of it, so it must not be important to his purpose in telling this portion of the story. However, it does seem curious, does it not? Regardless, they don't recognize him as their long-lost sibling. He has changed over the years, having become older and taking on the accouterments of the Egyptian lifestyle, and speaks to them in the Egyptian language through an interpreter. He knows who they are immediately, of course, giving him the distinct advantage. And, as we will see, he definitely seizes that advantage. What they do know is that strange things have been happening on their trip to Egypt, things that would be difficult, upon their return, to explain to their father Jacob. That is what sets up the drama in this part of the story.

The Egyptian governor had seemed to be inordinately interested in their family situation, but not before almost immediately charging them with being spies. "You have come to see the nakedness of the land!" he says to them accusingly. "No, no," they assure him, "we have just come to buy food, sent by our father, because the land is so bare" (Gen 42:10). Quickly they offer up the information that one brother remains back home with their father, while another has been lost and is "no more." The ten of them have come to procure food because of the famine. Of course, what they don't know is that they are providing information to the very one who already knows who they are and is completely aware of the situation.

Joseph decides not to let them off easily, whatever his motivation might have been. Revenge, perhaps? Or could it be his own sense of justice? His desire to be reunited with his loved ones? Whatever his purpose, it seems that he chooses to do so by making it as uncomfortable for his brothers as possible.

I'm not sure if this story is apocryphal or it actually happened, but I will pass it on regardless. It is said that during the Civil War a young northern soldier was caught committing a crime and was sentenced to death by hanging. The young man's mother managed to get an audience with President Lincoln, and begged for mercy. She was a widow, she explained, and her son was her only child. If he were to be hanged, she would be left all alone in the world.

Mr. Lincoln did indeed have pity on her and assured her that her son's life would be spared. As he escorted her from his office in the White House, he turned to her and said, "Nevertheless, madam, I do wish we could hang him just a little bit!"

Joseph's plan is to be reunited with his family. His motivation for doing so is to bring honor to the God who has seen him through some perilous times. But in the meantime, it appears he decides to hang his brothers just a little bit! He certainly doesn't make it easy for them. Keeping Simeon as collateral, he tells the remaining nine to go back home with their needed grain, then

The Baby of the Family

return to Egypt. That will be proof enough that they are not spies. And when they come back to retrieve Simeon, they are to bring Jacob's youngest son with them. That is not negotiable, he informs them. They are not to return without the baby of the family.

Along the way, they discover money in their sacks, funds they had taken to Egypt to pay for the grain. What is it doing in their grain bags? Now, the governor will think they are not only spies but thieves as well!

When they arrive back home, the sons of Jacob soon learn that their father will not hear of Joseph's demand, probably for more than one reason. He's already lost one son, Joseph, and it's quite possible he will never see Simeon again as he languishes in an Egyptian jail. Jacob will not risk Benjamin's life, not for all the grain in Egypt. No, no, no, no . . . no!

He takes all this very personally without taking any of the blame upon himself. "I am the one you have bereaved of children" (Gen 42:36), he says to his sons. Joseph isn't the only one who speaks accusingly, is he? "Joseph is no more, and Simeon is no more, and now you would take Benjamin. All this has happened to me! To me!"

There is a sense in which Jacob has always come across as self-centered. Think about it: He stole his brother's birthright so he might have it for himself, with the aid of his equally conniving mother. He tricked his father-in-law Laban and fled back home to the land of his fathers (though it could be said with justification that Laban deserved everything Jacob did to him). And even when he found himself in the dead of night wrestling with the messenger of God on the banks of the river Jabbok, Jacob refused to let go until he was blessed. Jacob was always looking for an edge, a way of seizing the advantage in any given situation. Now, in his old age, when life turns on him in the midst of this great famine, he blames his sons for his losses. The edge is gone and the only thing remaining is narcissism and self-pity. "All this has happened to *me*!"

Hunger, however, can be a great motivator, as well as life-changer. Once again, they have run out of grain, which is where we pick up this portion of the story. "Go again," Jacob says to his sons, pushing them toward Egypt, "buy us some more food" (Gen 43:2). He seems to say it in such a way that he fully expects his sons to obey his command... without question or argument.

Not this time. This time, the sons of Jacob tell their father, no.

So far in this narrative, Reuben has been the strong and more compassionate leader of the brothers. He is the one who wouldn't let them kill Joseph, and suggested they put him in the pit until they could figure out what to do with him. It was Reuben who bore the sad news to Jacob that his favored son Joseph was now "lost and is no more." It was Reuben who told his father that if they went back to Egypt with Benjamin, and did not bring him back upon their return, Jacob had his permission to kill his two sons as recompense. In this ongoing saga, generally when the brothers required a courageous spokesman, it was Reuben who stepped up to the plate and offered sibling leadership.

Interestingly, not this time. This time, it is Judah who speaks up. Yes, the very same Judah whose idea it was, years before, to sell Joseph into slavery rather than kill him. Perhaps still carrying the guilt of such a decision, he now finds it in himself to muster the courage to stand up to his stubborn father Jacob. He reminds his father of what the Egyptian governor had said to them. "The man solemnly warned us: 'You shall not see my face unless your brother (speaking of Benjamin, the baby of the family) is with you.' If you will send our brother with us," Judah says to his father Jacob, "we will go down and buy you food" (Gen 43:4).

Did you notice that? It's a fairly subtle turn of words, but it carries a lot of meaning. "If you will send our brother with us, we will go down and buy *you* food." Judah is letting his father know that they, he and his brothers, are not willing to shoulder all the blame for their unfortunate situation. Jacob has to admit to his part in it too. He's the one who favored Joseph and contributed to their resentment, a resentment that forced them to do what they had done so many years before. He's the one who, after Joseph was lost—and was "no more"—then placed his favor upon Benjamin because he was the only remaining son of Jacob's beloved wife Rachel. He, Jacob, is the one who, after they had returned from

The Baby of the Family

Egypt, was willing for Simeon to cool his heels in the Egyptian jail because he wouldn't allow Benjamin to go with his brothers to retrieve him.

The blame game is going to stop and it's going to stop right here and right now. "If you will not send him," Judah says to his father Jacob, "we will *not* go down" (Gen 43:5).

One of the all-time most popular television shows is *Bonanza*. Re-runs of this western can be viewed several times a day on multiple channels, and I admit I have seen just about all of them. I recall one day visiting a parishioner at a local nursing home. As I walked down the hall toward her room, I heard the unmistakable sound of the *Bonanza* theme song: "Dum diddy um diddy um diddy um diddy um dum, dum diddy um . . . " Sound familiar? Of course it does. It was all I could do to keep from entering the room to see which episode was playing! After all, I've just about seen them all.

The series starred Lorne Greene as the father Ben, and Pernell Roberts, Dan Blocker and Michael Landon as his three sons Adam, Hoss, and Little Joe. Pernell Roberts, a classically-trained actor who played the oldest son Adam, only stayed with the show six years despite its fourteen-year run. It is said that he left the show because he thought the storyline was ridiculous, that the program depicted an older man with three grown sons whom he still treated as if they were children who constantly had to defer to the wishes of their father despite the fact that they were adults.

I wonder if that might not have been something of the dynamic in the Jacob household, and Judah, acting like Pernell Roberts, finally decided he had had enough. "If you will not send him (referring to Benjamin, the baby of the family), we will not go down. Enough is enough!"

Resentment permeates the household of Jacob. There is no way to get around that. Ben—er, I mean Jacob—still isn't willing to let go of his resentment toward his sons, nor they from him. He's still taking this whole thing personally, as if this misfortune is his and his alone. "Why did you treat me so badly as to tell the man

61

that you had another brother? Why did you so readily offer such information?" Loose lips sink ships!

"The man (they still do not know Joseph's identity, remember) questioned us carefully about ourselves and our kindred . . . 'Is your father still alive? Have you another brother?'" (Gen 43:7).

"We had to answer his questions, don't you see?"

If he's going to defy the family patriarch, Judah needs to accept responsibility for his actions. Actually, when you think about it, showing more maturity than his father Jacob, Judah says, "Tell you what: send the boy (Benjamin, the baby of the family) with me (to Egypt) . . . " Judah does not say *us*, he says *me* . . . "I myself will be surety for him; you can hold me accountable for him. If I do not bring him back to you and set him before you alive and well, then let me bear the blame forever" (Gen 43:9).

But he doesn't stop there, does he? He gets in a bit of a dig toward his father, again revealing the resentment that has existed in this rather dysfunctional household for a lot of years. "If we had not delayed, we would now have returned twice" (Gen 43:10).

"If you had acted sensibly, it would all be over by now. As it is, it's time to put this show on the road!"

Jacob finally gives in. But to show that he's still the boss of this outfit, he starts barking orders, telling his sons what to pack and how to pack it, as well as how much money to take with them. Shades of Ben Cartwright! And then, possibly to show that he is willing to give up on at least some of the resentment he has shown them, he offers them a blessing: "May God Almighty (the Hebrew is what has become to us the familiar *El Shaddai*) grant you mercy before the man . . . " (Gen 43:14).

We have the advantage of knowing who all the players are, and of the intrigue that serves as the backdrop to this drama. As observers, we know what Jacob and his sons do not know. But in a real sense, that adds to the pathos of this situation. Jacob is not aware of the outcome, and can only place the final result of all this into the hands of *El Shaddai*, God Almighty, the very One with whom he had wrestled in the middle of the night so many years before. The remainder of his blessing is not only that God will grant mercy to his sons, but goes like this: "so that he (the Lord) may send back your other brother (referring to Simeon) and Benjamin (the baby of the family)" (Gen 43:14). Jacob seems to be telling God what to do as well!

Some things, especially when it comes to Jacob, never change.

And then, as Judah did with his father, Jacob gets in one final dig at his sons. He says, "As for me, if I am bereaved of my children, I am bereaved" (Gen 43:14). What will be will be. "If I lose my sons, let it be God's will." It's not very good theology, but it is a fairly effective guilt trip. A little guilt, you see, can go a long way, and it appears that Jacob is not hesitant to heap more than a little guilt on his sons as they depart for their second trip to Egypt.

It must have been a long and difficult journey to Egypt, for they do not know what the outcome will be once they arrive. If there is a place in this story that mirrors where we are in life, it is here. We do not know where our journey of life and faith will take us. Again, as we read this story of Jacob and his family, we are given the advantage of knowing what they have in mind, God's plans for them, and how their lives will conclude. And through the interpreted narrative of those who recorded this story, we are able to see God's intent in it all. As the sons of Jacob—not to mention Jacob himself—were willing to place their destiny in the hands of *El Shaddai*, so must we.

Since God can hit a straight lick with a crooked stick, let us learn from that old rascal Jacob. He did, whether from desperation or true faith—or a mixture of both—finally put this whole enterprise into the hands of God. Since we do not know the outcome of our story, don't you think it would be good for us to do the same?

Study/Thought Questions

1. How does Joseph take advantage of the situation? Is he fair toward his brothers? To what extent do you think revenge motivates him, if at all?

2. If you were writing this narrative, would you have included more details, more elements, to the story? If so, what would they be?

3. The author writes, "Joseph's plan is to be reunited with his family. His motivation for doing so is to bring honor to the God who has seen him through some perilous times." Which do you think is more important to Joseph?

4. Do you agree with the author when he portrays Jacob as self-centered? If not, why?

5. Do you relate to the evident dysfunction within the household of Jacob? Do you agree with the author in interpreting this situation in that light?

6. What does this portion of the story of Joseph teach you about your life?

The Silver Cup

"How can I go back to my father if the boy is not with me?"

GENESIS 44:34

When we are first introduced to the brothers of Joseph, we find them to be sullen and angry over their father's favoritism of him, to the point of hating Joseph and not speaking peaceably to him. Should we admit to having a certain amount of sympathy for them? After all, their collective anger is understandable. It would not have been a very pleasant way to live, knowing that your father obviously and overtly loved one of his sons more than you. Add to this dynamic the reality that Jacob has exhibited more love for Rachel than for your mother. You feel like a resented step-child whose sole purpose in life is to work for a father who, in many respects, looks less upon you as a son than perhaps a hired man. Each day the resentment would increase because it seems neither Jacob nor his favored son Joseph do anything to make life better for those who share their roof. It's been going on for seventeen years. That's a lot of time for their anger to build.

Adding to all this is that Joseph preens before his brothers in his nice, new coat, lording it over them at every opportunity, telling them of his dreams that revel in his superiority. No doubt, we would have been bitter too. By the time we first enter the Joseph story, their resentment toward him, and their father, has risen to murderous levels, and it doesn't take long for us to realize that something's got to give. The pressure has built up to the point that something—or someone—is going to explode. As we know, it finally does in the form of a pit, with Joseph eventually being sold into slavery by his brothers, his treasured coat covered in blood.

It could have been worse, you know. They had wanted to take his life. Now, *that* is anger!

When we encounter the portion of this story recorded in Genesis 44, a lot has changed in the intervening years. Let's consider for a moment what that is. First of all, Joseph is lost and is "no more." We are reminded of that repeatedly throughout this narrative. That statement is made over and over, not just for the purpose of stating what has happened, but to add to the sense of pain and loss in the heart and household of Jacob. It's as if every time we are told that Joseph is lost and "is no more," the grief and pain felt by Jacob is doubled since the previous reminder was given. Is that just as true of the brothers' guilt? Without a doubt, it serves as an important backdrop to the entire story. Joseph is lost and is "no more"—or so they think—and the grief and guilt builds and builds.

Perhaps it is the author's way of telling us just how much this tragic loss has impacted the family, possibly leading to even greater resentment on the part of Jacob's sons who can't seem to compete with Joseph even after he is gone. When they sold Joseph into slavery, they thought their troubles were over. But pits—both literal and figurative—are never deep enough to hide one's guilt. It is like Edgar Allen Poe's tell-tale heart. It just keeps beating louder and louder—THA-THUMP, THA-THUMP, THA-THUMP—until the sound of it is all you are able to hear.

Benjamin, somewhat, has taken Joseph's place in the affectionate eyes of their father. Jacob appears, at minimum, to be protective of the second "son of his old age." Apart from his grief, Jacob is the one person who doesn't appear to have changed that much. He still thinks mainly of himself, giving us the image of an old man who has grown ever more obstinate and unbending in his

The Silver Cup

latter years. Could it be because of the impact Joseph's loss has had on him? Unresolved grief is a terrible burden to bear . . .

. . . as is guilt. Guilt will indeed alter a person's life. This portion of the narrative focuses on the interaction between Joseph and his brothers, and guilt is the underlying factor.

On the surface, it appears that Joseph is enjoying his revenge just a little too much. The Hebrew scholar Gerhard von Rad says, referring to Joseph, "He is playing an insolent, almost wanton game with the brothers."[1] Already, he has placed the brothers in the position of having to stand against their father in demanding that on their second trip to Egypt they bring their baby brother Benjamin with them, something Jacob definitely did not want to happen. Already, Joseph has accused them of being spies, when he knows good and well they are not. Already, he has given them all a taste of what it is like to spend time in an Egyptian jail. Already, he has kept Simeon incarcerated while the brothers are sent back to Canaan. How long that has been, we do not know, but it was enough time for their grain finally to run out. Any length of time would be too long for poor Simeon, don't you think?

And now, Joseph pulls another fast one on them. It involves his personal silver cup. It appears to be more than just a drinking vessel. Joseph tells them he uses it for divination, so perhaps, not only does he drink from it, it functions as his crystal ball!

When we lived in Florida years ago, good friends from Baltimore sent us a bouquet of flowers as a house-warming gift. The flowers came in a colorful ceramic bowl. After the flowers were gone, I appropriated the bowl for my morning breakfast cereal, frosted mini-wheats being my cereal of choice. Over the years, I developed a real affection for that bowl. It became my favorite, not just for breakfast but for the occasional ice cream treat, don't you know. Not only was it just the right size, but every time I used it I thought of our friends Karen and John. I really loved that bowl. One morning, I dropped the bowl, breaking it beyond repair. After an appropriate period of mourning, I set out to find a new "favorite" bowl.

1. Von Rad, *Genesis*, 386.

We would soon be accompanying a group of senior adults on their trip to North Carolina. Knowing that shopping would be one of the major activities of the journey, one of my goals was to locate a new bowl. At every stop, I mentioned to the group that I was looking for a new cereal bowl, and just about everybody joined me in the search. They would bring me a bowl and ask if this could possibly be it. "No, no, it's just not right. But thank you, anyway." Eventually, I was successful in my search. In fact, I still have it, managing so far not to drop it on the kitchen floor, and use it almost daily. But I still miss the bowl given to us by our friends, and remember it with great fondness.

Was this silver cup Joseph's favorite? Was it given to him by a friend? A house-warming gift, perhaps? Did it indeed have some magical power from which he was able to do his divination, or did he just offer this as a possibility, a ruse, to deepen the intrigue? Who knows. What we do know is that he had his steward hide it in Benjamin's sack of grain, to be used as an excuse to haul his brothers back in order to exact more revenge on them.

But was it really revenge? Or was it a clever, if not divinely-inspired, plan by which the sons of Jacob would not only be reunited, but the guilt of the brothers could finally find resolution and forgiveness? Is this ultimately a story of redemption? You might guess that the latter is what we think truly happened.

The sons of Jacob hardly get beyond the city limits before they are overtaken by Joseph's steward. Despite the protests of the brothers, they are brought back to stand before the governor and give explanation for their "crime." They are so convinced of their innocence, however, that they tell the steward, "Should it (the silver cup) be found with any one of your servants, let him die; moreover the rest of us will become my lord's slaves" (Gen 44:9).

Uh oh. Methinks they spoke too soon. Beginning with the eldest son of Jacob, and going down the line, the sacks of grain were searched. No silver cup was found . . . until they came to Benjamin, the baby of the family. And there it was.

In this ancient world, tearing one's clothes was a sign of grief, despair, or repentance. When the silver cup was found in

The Silver Cup

Benjamin's belongings, his brothers immediately began tearing their garments. Theft was a very serious crime, generally calling for the death penalty. The narrator of the story does not tell us what they have to say, if anything. Maybe they know that by now words don't matter; they won't do any good, and cannot convey how they feel. The only thing they are left with is to tear their clothes.

Imagine what a sight it must have been as they came back to Joseph's home. Their clothing is like rags, hanging from their shoulders. Their heads are hung low in despair. Their faces show a real sense of desperation. After making all the promises to Jacob that Benjamin would be brought back home safely, they are now believing that he will be enslaved forever to this ruthless Egyptian ruler, the one who appears to have as much power as the Pharaoh himself.

I would imagine the thought crosses their minds that God Almighty (*El Shaddai*, remember) is doing this to them as recompense for the crime they committed years earlier in regard to their brother Joseph, the one who is lost and is "no more." There is no reason for them to think God is any less vengeful toward them than is the Egyptian governor. Guilt can lead to some pretty awful theology.

Speaking of God . . .

God is mentioned only once in this portion of Joseph's story (Gen 44:16). But this one occurrence says a great deal about the brothers, not to mention their limited theology. "God has found out the guilt of your servants," they say to Joseph. "God has *found out* . . . "? They make it sound like God is just now catching on to what has happened. It's like God has finally waked up and smelled the coffee! Do they not think that God has known all along? And did we mention that guilt can lead to some pretty awful theology? Yes, I think we did.

Maybe what they mean is, the thought has finally come to *them* that God might just have something to do with all this. Actions do have consequences, after all. Their guilt has been eating at them and eating at them all these years. They know they did wrong in selling their brother into slavery, and ever since that has been the underlying factor in everything they have experienced. Now, finally, what they did is coming to light, to the extent that they must at last pay for their crime. And not them only, but also Benjamin?! It's not fair! Benjamin had nothing to do with this. Why must he be the one to pay for their sins?!

Joseph, stretching out the agony just a bit more, informs Judah that Benjamin's life will not be forfeited. However, he will remain and be Joseph's slave. "But as for you," he says to Judah and his brothers, "go up in peace to your father" (Gen 44:17).

What?! "Go in peace to our father? You don't understand. If we do not return home with Benjamin, peace is the last thing we will have. Moreover, it will be the end of Jacob, our father. It will be the last straw for him. We can't go home, not without the baby of the family." It is then that Judah, once again speaking for the brothers, offers his life in exchange for Benjamin's.

Leslie Weatherhead, pastor of the London Temple during the Second World War, tells of his military service in India. One day, he observed workers as they sewed oriental rugs. Occasionally, he noticed one would make a mistake. But rather than tear out the thread and start over, the skillful worker would continue, creating a design around the flawed stitch.

That became a parable for him, that when we do wrong God does not require that we go back for a "do-over." Instead, God chooses to continue weaving in our lives, so that our mistakes become a part of the final design. If that is indeed true, is that not what God has chosen to do in this fascinating account of Joseph and his brothers? While the brothers, returning to Egypt with their torn clothing, think all is lost, instead God has chosen to use this as an opportunity for reunion and redemption. And if that was true of Joseph and his brothers, is it not possible for you and me as well?

The journey of life and faith comes with baggage. In that baggage you will often find guilt, the consequences of our actions, and sometimes torn clothing, heartbreak and tears. But it also comes with redemption. It may be hard to see it at the time, when it is occurring, yet the promise of it is ours to take to heart. It is best we do not try to figure out how or maybe even why. Just accept that it is so. Only then can we bask in the glow of God's grace, realizing that it is nothing we do of ourselves. It is freely given by a God who has not just "found out" what is going on inside our hearts, but has been the driving force behind it all the time.

The next time you find that proverbial silver cup in your grain bag, and your heart leaps into your throat because you know that all your sins have been found out, trust that God, the Master Weaver, has a plan of redemption in store for you. You don't have to know what it is, at least not at the time. Faith doesn't come with a silver cup used for divination. But you will know it when it does eventually come to you. Right now, it is enough to believe that such an outcome is in God's hands.

So, let me ask you: is there any other place you would want it to be?

Study/Thought Questions

1. Do you have any sympathy for the sons of Jacob?
2. How do grief and guilt go together?
3. Do you agree with Gerhard Von Rad that Joseph "is playing an insolent, almost wanton game with the brothers"?
4. The planting of the silver cup was ingenious. But was it divinely-inspired or cruel revenge?
5. The author describes the scene of Jacob's sons returning to Egypt to "face the music" with the authorities. How would you depict this event?
6. The author says, "Guilt can lead to some pretty awful theology." Do you agree?
7. In your life, what would you like to do over? Knowing that is not possible, how has God woven redemption, using your flaws as material and thread?

Reunion

"It was not you who sent me here, but God..."

∾ GENESIS 45:8 ∾

Joseph has proven himself to be quite clever in keeping his identity secret from his brothers. It may not have been that difficult. They were hardly expecting ever to see him again, and certainly not under these circumstances. Nevertheless, he takes full advantage of the situation.

For some time, Joseph has been toying with them, stringing them along, requiring that they confront their father Jacob in order to bring Benjamin, his younger brother, to Egypt with them. Do you wonder what Joseph's motivation might have been for doing all this? I have a theory, if you would like to hear it. Perhaps he has done so in order to see for himself if they have truly changed in all the years that have come and gone since they had treated him so badly as to sell him into slavery.

The last time he had seen them, prior to their coming to Egypt seeking grain, was when they had put him in that pit in Dothan. There's been a lot of water under the bridge since that time. Enough time for them to regret what they did so many years before? That's what Joseph wants to know.

When people experience extreme trauma, whether the sudden and unexpected loss of a loved one or an event they know will indeed change their lives forever, they react generally in one of at least two ways. Sometimes, the hurt itself shields their minds from memory, so that they never can consciously recall what happened or how they felt in that moment. Oddly enough, others remember every little detail: what they were doing when they first discovered or experienced what happened, how everything smelled, what sounds were present, if any. My guess is that the raw memory of that fateful day, even after all these years, still lingers vividly in Joseph's mind, indelibly printed into his long-term memory.

They had ripped his coat from off him, the fancy garment given him by his father Jacob, and then callously sat around eating their lunch while he languished in that hole in the ground. The biblical account doesn't tell us this, but we can guess that they taunted him all the while, letting him know what they thought of him and his behavior. Daddy wasn't around to protect him anymore, so they had nothing to lose in informing him of their intense hatred of him.

Apparently, it wasn't just jealousy that motivated them to behave this way. They were "up to here" with his childish and selfish behavior, his blatant feelings of superiority. No one likes to feel they have second-class status, especially within one's own family. According to the way the story is told, their hatred of Joseph was quite real, and, though we may not approve of their actions, was fairly understandable. Joseph must have been an insufferable pain in the neck, and hard to be around.

Still, it's difficult for us to understand why they would go to such drastic measures. They really were planning to kill him, you see, so putting him in that pit was Plan B. Plan A had been to take his life, and the only thing that prevented them from doing so was Judah's intercession on Joseph's behalf. "What profit is it if we kill our brother and conceal his blood?" (Gen 37:26). "What profit is it . . . ?"

Let's focus on that word *profit*.

It can be taken at least two different ways. Judah could have been referring to the eventual consequences they would face back home if they killed Joseph. Nothing good would come to them—no emotional profit, as it were—if they murdered their little brother, except perhaps, not having to put up with his fanciful dream interpretations and his constant boasting of superiority over them. They obviously wouldn't miss that, but would the guilt of it be too heavy a price to pay?

Their belief in God might not have been very strong, but they *did* believe in God. Would it not be possible for God to exact revenge for Joseph's murder? There would be no emotional, no spiritual, no personal profit in taking Joseph's life, especially if their father Jacob discovered what they had done. If that ever happened, there would be you-know-what to pay. Did they want to face such a prospect?

Or, Judah could have been thinking quite literally. Frankly, the following statement seems to support that understanding. It appears that Judah is wanting to profit financially from the situation by selling his brother. If they kill him, they will not be able to gain from his loss. Joseph is worth nothing to them if he is dead. Slavery was an active industry in those days and in that part of the world, and circumstances have landed right in their laps for them to take financial advantage of it. "Come, let us sell him to the Ishmaelites," Judah says, "and not lay our hands on him." Then, showing some element of human kindness—not much, but some—he says, "For he *is* our brother, our own flesh." (Gen 37:27).

Now, after all these years have passed—now that the tables have been turned and he is in control of the situation—Joseph is attempting to see if his brothers are the same as they had been so many years before when they agreed to sell him into slavery, and profit from it. Could they still be as ruthless today as they had been back then? Had they the opportunity to do it all over again—get rid of their little brother—would they do it? The best way for him to find the answers to those questions is to observe how they treat Benjamin, and the only way that could happen is for him to hide his identity while putting them to the test. When Joseph tells them to go back home to Jacob, but to leave Benjamin there in Egypt to be his slave, Judah, serving as the brothers' spokesman once again, says to him, "How can I go back to my father if the boy (Benjamin)

REUNION

is not with me? I fear to see the suffering that would come upon my father" (Gen 44:34).

Judah, who years before was hardly worried about what his father Jacob might think, and was ready to kill Joseph before Reuben convinced the brothers to spare his life, is now thinking not of himself but of his father and his little brother, apparently seeking their welfare above his own. It is a striking development, considering the kind of person Judah appeared once to have been.

What kind of person *had* Judah been? The thirty-eighth chapter of Genesis provides us a fairly clear answer to that question.

After the story is told of the brothers selling Joseph into slavery, there is a bit of an interlude (chapter thirty-eight), the purpose of which is to give us some insight into Judah and the kind of person he was. I'll give you a hint: of the sons of Jacob, he is hardly the most redemptive. Perhaps this story is included so we can see later the change that has come over him as this fascinating narrative commences.

Judah knows what it means to grieve, having lost two of his sons, as well as his wife. How he responds to these losses seems hardly appropriate, but we remind you that these are crude people who looked at life from a different perspective than do we. If you are interested in following Judah's story, I recommend you read the thirty-eighth chapter of Genesis, and you will see what I mean. After doing so, you will come away with the definite feeling that when we see Judah in this portion of the story, as Joseph is reunited with his brothers, he is indeed a different person. Judah has changed. And quite frankly, Judah *needed* to change!

But so has Joseph. He is not the same immature teenager he was before, the one who took such blatant advantage of his father's favoritism toward him. And it has to do with more than just the passing of time. It was what he had experienced over the years, and how he responded to it. Let's explore that for a moment.

We don't know how long he had been in that pit before the brothers sold him into slavery. Several hours, perhaps? It was while they were eating that they first spied the caravan of Ishmaelite traders, and the idea came to Judah to sell Joseph to them. We made the case earlier that it may have taken Joseph a while to realize his brothers were deadly serious—*deadly* being the operative word—in their efforts to get rid of him. But it may have been long enough for him finally to start thinking about the serious implications of what was happening to him. And then, on the journey from Dothan to Egypt, where he was bought by Potiphar, the Pharaoh's captain of the guard, surely he had the time for introspection, to think about why this has happened to him and what he might do as a result, especially since his life has become so unalterably changed—and so quickly.

By the time he is placed in Potiphar's household, we see that Joseph is making the best of his situation. Eventually, he is elevated to a position of trust, yet soon we find him needing to avoid the amorous advances of Potiphar's lecherous wife. When that situation turns against him, he is thrown into prison because of her false testimony.

What does all this mean? Why is Joseph going through these trials? One result from all this is, he has plenty of time to think—and no doubt to pray. Whatever his concept of God might have been, it appears that Joseph never considered himself to be alone and left to his own devices, that his God had a purpose in mind for all the things that have happened to him, and has not, under any circumstances, deserted him. It was a belief that sustained Joseph in the darkest of times, and brought him to this position of status and authority in Pharaoh's court.

That thought continues with the story we are considering now. It is what motivated him to refrain from immediately identifying himself to his brothers. God has yet to make known to him the divine purpose in all this, and he waits patiently to discover the Lord's intent before he offers his brothers, to use today's television terminology, "the big reveal."[1]

The sons of Jacob may be clueless as to what is going on, but Joseph gradually sees how it is all unfolding, and in faith he places it in God's hands. Once he has divulged his identity to them, and they finally discover that the governor of Egypt is none other than

1. Cartledge, "Selling Joseph," *Nurturing Faith*, July–Aug 2017, 36.

their long-lost brother Joseph, he says to them, "It was not you who sent me here (to Egypt), but God; he has made me a father to Pharaoh, and lord of all his house and ruler over all the land of Egypt" (Gen 45:8). One thing for sure, Jacob's ego is still intact!

"It was not you who sent me here, but God . . . "

How does that statement strike you? Does Joseph believe that God is behind every human action, determining what happens so God might then use those circumstances to God's advantage and will? We need to be careful in thinking along those lines because it is indeed a slippery theological slope.

For example, in the last few years Texas, Florida and the Carolinas have been ravaged by hurricanes. Mexico, Japan and Nicaragua have experienced deadly earthquakes. Entire cities in California have been consumed by wildfires. Almost daily we read of natural disasters that have claimed numerous lives and caused tremendous loss of property. The year 2020 closed with the highest number of Covid-19 cases to date, resulting in more than 300,000 deaths just in the United States. Did God cause these things to happen so God could then come through after the fact and show God's power and will?

Again, let's be careful. Some people think along these lines, but let's not join their ranks. There have been stories revealed to us of how some folks have acted courageously and compassionately in assisting those who were victims of the storms or pandemic. In the wake of 2017's Hurricane Maria, one cruise vessel, full of vacationing passengers, turned into a mercy ship when many of the passengers volunteered to help evacuate those who lost their homes. We can suggest that their actions were motivated by a desire, planted in their hearts by God, to be of service to their fellow human beings, and I would agree with that. But did God cause the storms in order for that to happen? I'm not so willing to go there!

Apart from natural occurrences such as storms and earthquakes, is God to blame for human evil? Sometimes, Paul's admonition that "all things work together for good to those who love God" (Rom 8:28) seems to ring hollow and untrue. How do we reconcile that?

Why don't we look at it this way... What does God do best, especially in situations like this, like the one that Joseph finds himself in with his brothers? What does this reunion of Jacob's sons tell us? I would suggest to you that it reveals our God is One who chooses to take what happens to us and transform it into God's plan of redemptive grace. God takes our pain and turns it toward the divine purpose, sees our grief and bends it toward God's grace, is there with us when we stumble and picks us up so we might continue in the journey toward redemption.

"It was not you who sent me here," Joseph says to his brothers, "but God..." It takes spiritual insight to be able to see the big picture of what God might possibly have in store, and conclude how God is in it. It certainly takes a spirit of humility and openness, a heart of faith that always leaves open the door for God to come in.

It is not surprising that Joseph, when it comes time for him to reveal his identity, would be overcome with emotion. We can only imagine how his brothers might have felt. And did you notice what was said of Jacob when his sons returned home and told him that Joseph was alive? His spirit, we are told, was *revived*. Not only has God kept Benjamin safe, but will soon reunite Jacob's entire family. He couldn't have possibly asked for anything more.

What will it take for our spirit to be revived? Is there a reunion in our future? An opportunity for forgiveness to take place? For resentment to be replaced by redemption? Do you find yourself in need of a "cleansing, life-giving experience" like the one we find in Jacob's family?[2]

As ancient as is this story of Joseph's reunion with his brothers, the need for such a thing to happen again is as fresh as this morning's news. I encourage you to explore your life and heart, and see if there is a need for you to open yourself to such a possibility. It might just be the best thing that ever happens to you. There is one thing for sure: God is in that kind of experience, and is more than ready to be there with you and for you when you give your life to what God has in store.

2. Cartledge, 36.

REUNION

Study/Thought Questions

1. How have Joseph's brothers changed over the years since they put him in the pit?
2. Do you think Joseph's brothers might have remembered the details of that fateful day as vividly as does he?
3. What do you think Judah meant by the word *profit*?
4. According to Judah's response to Joseph (Genesis 45:34), he seems to be thinking more of his father and his brother Benjamin than he is of himself. To what extent does this show a change of heart on his behalf?
5. A central theme of the Joseph narrative is that in all his experiences God has a plan in mind, not only for Joseph, but for the people of Israel. Do you believe that? What are the theological consequences of such a belief?
6. Consider the calamities we have experienced these last few years. Have you seen God's presence and purpose in any of it? If so, how?

Wagon Train

"Joseph's own hand shall close your eyes"

GENESIS 46:4

How long had it been since Jacob had settled in the land of Canaan? We can't know for sure, but that's the word that is used for it—"settled." It carries a lot of meaning, doesn't it? *Settled.* If you were to describe where you are in life right now, would you use the word "settled"? If you're not sure, think of what it would take for you to pack up and move somewhere else.

I recall the day my brother Hugh and I brought our parents to Little Rock for mental evaluation, knowing that due to their increasing dementia they would never return home. A few months later, after having placed them in a nursing home, it fell to us to go back to our hometown and clean out their house in order to put it on the market.

It was a five-acre homestead on the outskirts of town. Situated on what was early-on a gravel road, it came complete with a pre-Civil War era barn constructed of rough-hewn yellow poplar logs. Dad simply and always called it "The Place." He was forever working on it . . . fixing this, fixing that. I was not yet five years old when we moved there in the spring of 1954, which means they lived in that place more than fifty years. Talk about settled! The next spring, when we cleaned out the house—and sadly tore down the barn, due to safety concerns—we found out firsthand just how settled our parents had become.

When you live in one location long enough, it becomes a part of your identity and is embedded in your soul. I wonder if that's the way Jacob felt about the land of Canaan, Hebron to be more exact.

Over lunch one time, a friend and I were discussing events that had occurred since we were last together. As we talked, he told me that a mutual friend asked if he would like to buy their house. "You've sold your home?" my friend asked him. "Yes, we bought another one a few blocks away." My response was, "Does he know that it's harder to move a few blocks than it is to move across the country?"

It's true. I know by personal experience. Once you've settled somewhere, it's difficult to pack up and relocate, even if it's just down the street.

How long have you lived in your current place of residence? My wife Janet and I have been in our home more than eighteen years, and the thought of ever having to leave it makes me shudder inside. In fact, my theology of hell has nothing to do with sulphur and eternal flames. It is a moving van! Thinking that I would have to prepare my house for sale gives me cold chills.

Yet, that is what Jacob and his clan are doing as we encounter them in this passage we read earlier. Jacob would no doubt be excited at the prospect of getting to see his beloved son Joseph again, the son who for so very long he thought was "lost and is no more." With the expectation of seeing his long-lost son, Jacob is more than happy to load up his family of sixty-six (!) people, less his daughters-in-law (for some reason, the author of this account almost goes out of his way to let us know they don't count). I do think, however, that Jacob let them go along for the ride. It's just that they don't count in the final tally for some reason. Jacob packs up "all that he had" (Gen 46:1) and heads out for Egypt. It is a relatively simple statement to make (they just packed up and left), but think of how very hard it must have been to do.

When my brother and I drove from our parents' home that November day in 2006, we knew they would never see "The Place" again. They didn't know that, which of course added to our sense of guilt for doing this, a feeling I carry with me to this day. Jacob was very much aware that when he returned to Canaan, it would be in a box. He was, after all, a realist. He knew he would never see Hebron again. The only thing he had left to look forward to in life was seeing Joseph before he died.

It is impossible to know Jacob's state of mind, but G. Henton Davies says something that I think must have been true: "However great was his desire to see Joseph, he (Jacob) cannot even have contemplated such a journey, or indeed have set out, without great misgivings."[1] How does Davies know this? Well, it does not take a lot of keen insight to be able to read between the lines—not in this case.

Jacob's wagon train has traveled southwest from Hebron to Beer-sheba, a distance of about thirty miles. He stopped there and "offered sacrifices to the God of his father Isaac" (Gen 46:1). I may be reading too much into it, but did you notice that he didn't offer these sacrifices to *his* God, but to the God of his father Isaac? Is that just an expression, or does it have a deeper, perhaps theological, meaning?

In order to make any sense of this, we have to re-visit the story of Jacob's father Isaac for a moment. He was, as was his father Abraham, a bit of a nomad. In fact, at one point, as did Abraham with Sarah, Isaac pawned off his wife Rebekah as his sister in order to, in his way of thinking, guarantee their safety. His travels found him in Beer-sheba, and it was there that the God of his father Abraham spoke to him and said, "Do not be afraid, for I am with you and will bless you . . . " (Gen 26:24).

Beer-sheba. And now, years later, Isaac's son Jacob, in his old age, finds himself as he journeys to Egypt, at Beer-sheba. Evidently, having been told the story of his father's experience there, Jacob stops the wagon train and offers sacrifices to the God of his father Isaac. That doesn't mean that he worships God only because he

---

1. Davies, *Broadman Bible Commentary*, 285.

has inherited this God from his father and grandfather. He understands the circumstances that have brought him to this place. It is holy ground. Wherever we encounter God, especially in the place where our ancestors have been, it is indeed a sacred place.

Whenever you find yourself unsure of where you are going, or what the future might hold, or for whatever reason you are afraid, it is your Beer-sheba. It is holy ground, the place where you will hear God say to you one of the most constant refrains in all of scripture, "Do not be afraid." God said it to Isaac, and now repeats the admonition to Jacob as he makes his way to Egypt. "Do not be afraid."

"Jacob, Jacob." God repeats, when God calls Jacob by name. It may have been just a literary effect, designed by the author as a way of letting the reader know that God is drawing Jacob into conversation. The same device is used when God visits the boy Samuel (1 Samuel 3:4). But there could be another possibility. Sometimes Jacob got so caught up in his own thoughts and schemes—and possibly his fears—that he blocked out other voices. So God calls his name twice, to get his attention. "Jacob . . . oh Jacob." Finally, Jacob responds. "Here I am, Lord, I'm listening." "I am God, the God of your father; do not be afraid . . . do not be afraid to go down to Egypt, for I will make of you a great nation there. I myself will go down with you to Egypt, and I will also bring you up again; and Joseph's own hand shall close your eyes" (Gen 46:4).

It is God's promise that, while Jacob will never see his homeland again, Egypt will not be his final resting place. It will be the place of his family's reunion, where Jacob will once again see his beloved son Joseph. Once that reunion takes place, and the famine is over, Jacob will return home to the land of his ancestors where he will be buried next to his loved ones.

As Yogi Berra would say, it is *deja vu* all over again! The same promise given to Abraham, and then to Isaac, is offered to Jacob as well, in his old age when his life is fragile and his misgivings and fears are great. This is not a regional God who stops at the borders of our fears and wishes us well as we go alone into the unknown. This is the God who comes to us in the midst of our greatest fears and misgivings, no matter what they are or where they are, and says, "I will be with you."

 I once heard Daniel Grant explain whimsically how God led him to be president of Ouachita Baptist University, my alma mater. Dr. Grant was at Vanderbilt, another of my former schools, when the Lord spoke to him. "Daniel, I want you to leave Nashville and Vanderbilt and go to Arkadelphia, Arkansas, and be president of Ouachita Baptist University." Daniel said to the Lord, "Let me think about it." So, he prayed about it, and eventually said to the Lord, "I have thought about it and have decided this: I will leave Nashville and go to Arkadelphia if you promise to go with me." The Lord responded, "Let me think about it." After a while the Lord appeared to Daniel once again and repeated his refrain about leaving Vanderbilt to go to Ouachita. "Will you go with me?" Daniel asked. And the Lord said, "I've thought about it. I'll go with you as far as Memphis."

 That is obviously not how God works. God is willing to accompany Jacob, even to Egypt.

 Interestingly enough, after all of the dramatic events leading up to this very moment—the coat, the pit, Joseph taken into slavery only to rise and fall and rise again in the courts of Pharaoh, the trickery toward his brothers and demands that Benjamin be brought to Egypt only for Joseph to once again make demands of his brothers while continuing to conceal his identity—after all the drama presented in this fascinating saga, not much is made of the reunion between Joseph and his father Jacob. There is a great deal more intrigue earlier in the story when Joseph first recognizes his brothers and then toys with them before finally letting them know who he was. Here, the drama is rather subdued. Joseph kneels before his father and weeps . . . and weeps and weeps . . . "a good while," we are told, "a good while" (Gen 46:29). Somehow, that's drama enough, don't you think?

 In explaining this, Clyde Francisco says, "The occasion was too sacred for words."[2] We are left with our imaginations to figure out what kind of occasion it must have been, if for no other reason

---

2. Francisco, *Broadman Bible Commentary*, 273–274.

than we are told only that Joseph wept. Nothing is said of Jacob's response, only that now having seen his beloved son, he is prepared to die . . . "since," he says, "I have seen your face and know that you are still alive" (Gen 46:30). After all these years of not knowing, of wondering, of thinking that Joseph was lost and is no more, only now to see him face-to-face, perhaps all of Jacob's tears had already been used up.

The last time Frances Taylor saw her brand-new husband, G.D., he was riding in the back of a pick-up truck with other fellow recruits as they drove away. The year was 1943, and the United States was in the midst of a great world war. After G.D. completed basic training he would make his way to the Pacific where he served the United States Marine Air Corps as a pilot. Frances was pregnant with their son when he left for war. Somewhere over the ocean, on one of his missions, G.D.'s plane disappeared and neither he nor his plane were ever found. Fifty-nine years later, on August 8, 2002, we held his memorial service in Russellville, Arkansas, and his "burial" in the Old Baptist Cemetery north of town, with full military honors.

Frances told me it took so long to have G.D.'s service because his mother, as long as she was alive, never gave up hope that someday he might return. Every time a car drove up in her driveway, Frances explained, her mother-in-law wondered if it might not be her son who had finally come home.

Does that story help you somehow in putting yourself in Jacob's place in an attempt to feel how he might have felt? Despite the bloody coat brought back to Jacob by his other sons, as their "proof" that Joseph had been killed by a wild animal, did Jacob, all those years, wonder if Joseph might not be alive and would come back home to him again? Every time a cart or horse—a camel, perhaps—approached the house, did Jacob think it might be his long-lost son who has come home? Now, having received word that Joseph is indeed alive, he is going to Egypt to be with him. And when he finally sees Joseph's face, and reaches out to touch him, the moment is too sacred for words and Jacob is too spent for tears.

My mother was the next to the youngest of seven siblings. One of those was her older brother Cecil. Cecil was the mystery person in the family. One day, as a relatively young man, and long before I was born, when mother was still quite young, Cecil simply disappeared. The family heard nothing from him for years and years. Occasionally, his name would come up in my mother's conversations with her siblings—usually centered around wondering where he might be or if he was alive—and why he had left in the first place.

When I was about ten years old or so, my mother received a phone call one day from her oldest sister Roena, the one everyone referred to as Aunt Sook. Cecil was coming home, she told Mom. She had heard from Cecil and he was coming home! Could the family get together to welcome him? After all these years, Cecil was coming home!

I still remember it. We gathered at Aunt Sook's and Uncle Arlon's home at 714 South Sixth Street in my hometown of Paragould, Arkansas. I don't recall much of that evening, except for a couple of things. I met Uncle Cecil, shook his hand and tolerated his tousling my hair . . . not that I had much, since in those days I wore the old flattop haircut. Remember those? He probably got pomade on his hand—or "butch wax" we called it—the stuff we put on our hair to make it stand up straight. I remember him sitting in Uncle Arlon's favorite chair and thinking this must indeed be a special occasion because I didn't recall Uncle Arlon ever giving up that chair for anybody, no matter who they might have been. Uncle Cecil patiently answered questions about where he had been and what he had done, and seemed to enjoy being the center of attention.

Truth be told, I think he was what used to be referred to as a hobo. The word my dad used for him was *bum*. He spent a lot of time around the trains, and I don't think he was in the habit of paying for a ticket, if you know what I mean.

And then, the next day Cecil left. He just left, never to be seen by the family again.

Wagon Train

That would not be Jacob's experience. God had made him a promise that upon his death "Joseph's own hand" (Gen 46:4) would close his eyes. It may seem to us a rather strange assurance, but Jacob took it for the way it was meant. After a long life of struggle and uncertainty, of gain and loss, of hope and fear, faith and doubt (sound familiar?) Jacob would go to his grave with his family reunited, with Joseph at his side.

As the wagon train gets closer to Egypt and to the family reunion with Joseph, Jacob sends his eldest son Judah on ahead. The Hebrew expression means, "to show the way before him." Judah had of course been that way before, at least twice, in his efforts to secure grain for his family. Jacob had never been here before, so he sends Judah ahead of the wagon train to be the scout.

None of us, in our journey of life and faith, has ever been here before. We're not speaking of a physical location. We're thinking of time. We've never been in this time—this moment—before, and as we continue inexorably through life, Jacob's experiences tell us we can look to God for the assurances that wherever we are, and whenever we are, God is at our side, showing us the way before us. Let us be assured that wherever our respective journeys take us, God will not stop at the border but will accompany us on the way, wherever the way takes us.

It is an assurance we need, and one that is given to us. It requires faith to take that promise into our hands and our hearts, that God has chosen to bless us. It is indeed a good thought, don't you agree?

Study/Thought Questions

1. What does it mean for you to be "settled"?
2. What misgivings (the term employed by G. Henton Davies) did Jacob have when he left Canaan?
3. What is your Beer-sheba?
4. Why do you think God calls Jacob's name twice?

5. Where and when has God come to you in the midst of your fears?

6. Have you ever had a reunion that was "too sacred for words" (Clyde Francisco)?

7. The author describes Jacob's life and God's final gift of grace to him. Can you try to imagine what was going through Jacob's mind and heart as his caravan makes its way to Egypt?

8. Of all his sons, why do you think Jacob sent Judah ahead to be his scout?

9. Do you believe God is by your side as you journey through life?

Favor

"The time of Israel's death drew near"

GENESIS 47:29

ABRAHAM, Isaac, and Jacob. The Hebrew Triumvirate, the Big Three, the first of the great fathers of the faith. Forever after, when the Jews identified themselves, they said first and foremost that they worshiped the God of Abraham, Isaac, and Jacob.

Where does that leave Joseph, the Dream Catcher? After all, this book is devoted to him and his story. Tony Cartledge points out that "while we normally think of (this section of Genesis) as the story of Joseph, the text is careful to tell us it is the story of *Jacob's* family."[1] G. Henton Davies, who was cited in the previous chapter, goes so far as to say that next to Abraham, Isaac, and Jacob, "even Joseph is a poor fourth."[2]

And yet, once we are told that this is the account of Jacob (aka Israel) and his family, the scene immediately shifts to the seventeen-year-old Joseph, his receiving the special coat from his father, and the ensuing difficulty with his angry brothers who eventually put him into a pit and then sell him into slavery. There is one exception, the previously-cited chapter (thirty-eight) that diverts from the Joseph narrative and tells us the misfortunes and

1. Cartledge, 34.
2. Davies, *Broadman Bible Commentary*, 290.

misdeeds of his brother Judah. But once again, and rather quickly, the storyline comes back dutifully to Joseph and his adventures. All in all, judging from the way the narrative goes, you would think that Jacob is being left in Joseph's dust as we follow his adventures in Egypt. But that is not what happens, is it? Finally, we are brought back to Jacob when Joseph is reunited with his family. It is at this point that the narrative seems to be refocused on the old patriarch and takes a dramatic turn when Jacob, knowing he is about to die, seeks the favor of his son Joseph.

Does the way this story is put together seem odd to you somehow? Frankly, it does to me.

There is another problem, it seems. As we come nearer to the conclusion of the narrative, not to mention Jacob's life, what we know of Jacob causes us to think that he just doesn't seem to be the type to ask a favor of anyone, especially one of his sons, even his favorite son from whom he was separated so many years and with whom he is now reunited.

Perhaps this all comes about because seventeen years after migrating from Canaan to Egypt due to the famine, Jacob still finds himself in this foreign land. Admittedly, Egypt has been good to him. He has gained many possessions, we are told. He and his family "were fruitful and multiplied exceedingly" (Gen 47:27). And, he is very much aware that his son Joseph is one of the major players in Pharaoh's court.

All in all, Jacob has little or nothing to complain about. Could it be that he has come to know his place in the scheme of things, that he has prospered in Egypt largely because of his son's position and ability to provide him a place where he can thrive? And so, as he comes near the end of his life and he needs to make arrangements for his final resting place, despite all that Egypt has offered him, Jacob seeks from his son the assurance that he will not be buried in foreign soil but will be returned to the land of his fathers. "If I have found favor with you," he says to Joseph, "put your hand under my thigh and promise to deal loyally and truly with me" (Gen 47:29).

Favor

What? Did Jacob think Joseph would do otherwise? After all the years of separation, the effort finally to bring his family safely to Egypt so they might not starve in Canaan, after all he has gone through to secure reconciliation with his family, forgiving his brothers for what they had done to him by selling him into slavery, did Jacob really think Joseph was going to throw all that away by doing anything *but* deal loyally and truly with his father? Judah might do such a thing, maybe, even Reuben, perhaps. But not Joseph. If Jacob hadn't learned the lesson by now, when would he? Joseph has always been, and always shall be, loyal and true to his word! What was Jacob thinking?

It appears that this entire scene, this "favor" Jacob asks of Joseph, takes place to fulfill Joseph's original dream. Do you remember? Jacob's asking a favor of his son is making complete what Joseph had envisioned so many years before, when, as a seventeen year-old he dreamt that not only would his brothers bow down before him, so would his father. It was one thing for him to dream all this, and something entirely different for him to tell them about it. Needless to say, it did not help relationships in the family of Jacob, whose story, we remind you, is being told in these pages.

Who does the young Joseph think his father is, anyway? He's one of the Big Three! The God Joseph serves so faithfully, remember, is the God of Abraham, Isaac, and Jacob, not the God of Abraham, Isaac, and Joseph! Maybe that is why the "favor" that Jacob asks of Joseph is really more of a demand. "Put your hand under my thigh and promise to deal loyally and truly with me," the old and dying patriarch says to his son. And Joseph dutifully does as his father asks.

In an age when vows don't seem to mean much, except when they are made and then easily forgotten or broken, it may be difficult for us to understand all this. But in the days of Jacob, such vows were lifelong and binding, as solid as a legal contract and maybe even more so. After all, Jacob, with the assistance of his scheming mother Rebekah, went to great lengths to secure his father's birthright, knowing that once he was able to wrest it away from his slightly older twin brother Esau, it could never be taken from him. It would be his forever. That birthright was the equivalent of a solemn vow, emphasis on the word *solemn*.

Back in those days, vows were eternal, though a case could be made that Jacob never felt secure in the promise of his birthright. For many years, he kept looking over his shoulder wondering if maybe he had gained the favor improperly, and God would not honor it. Why else would he demand that the angel with whom he wrestled at Jabbok bless him before Jacob would be willing to release him from his grasp? Is this Jacob's way of wrestling with Joseph, his own son?

A psychological analysis of Jacob's life might yield some very interesting results, not the least of which is a streak of insecurity. Just about everywhere Jacob turned, he sought the advantage, or insisted on being blessed. That may have led to the scene we read about a bit earlier when he requires his son Joseph—repeatedly—to make his vow to him.

There is something of a parallel to this in the New Testament. Speaking of the Big Three, how about Peter, James, and John? If Joseph is a poor fourth to Abraham, Isaac, and Jacob, is there a New Testament counterpart to Joseph? How about Paul? Though most of the New Testament epistles are attributed to the self-appointed apostle, there is an interesting story found in the Acts of the Apostles that reveals he was not necessarily held in high esteem by all his peers, especially those in Jerusalem.

Paul is insistent on going to the Holy City, despite the fact that not only is he disliked by the local church leadership, he will be endangered by others who see him as a political threat. At every stop along the way he is urged by his fellow believers and supporters not to go there. His life will be in danger in Jerusalem, he is told repeatedly.

"I am ready," he says to them stubbornly, "not only to be bound but even to die in Jerusalem for the name of the Lord Jesus" (Acts 21:13). Once he arrives, he is greeted warmly by the church leadership, we are told. That is the word that is used—*warmly*—though what follows seems to belie that notion somewhat. Is it possible to be greeted warmly and at the same time cautiously? The two don't seem to go together, do they?

The leaders of the church in Jerusalem have not yet come to the point that they are willing to give up their commitment to the old Jewish ways, primarily of circumcision and their adherence to the law. Paul's behavior—his insistence that Gentiles not be bound to Jewish customs in order to follow Jesus—in their minds is a threat to their traditions, and they are still at a place where their religious customs are vital to them.

We lived six years in Nashville, Tennessee. We found Nashville, as you might expect, to be unique in its culture. The two major industries were religion and country music. Several denominational headquarters were housed there, and you could pretty much find a church or two on just about every street corner, it seemed. In those days, one of the prominent downtown congregations was going through a rancorous split. The *Nashville Tennessean* newspaper published a five-part series on the church's struggles, complete with naming the people involved, and airing all the church's dirty laundry for the public to see and read. Religion is big business in the Tennessee capital . . .

. . . as is country music. When Tammy Wynette and George Jones split, everyone knew about it, and why. Dolly Parton and Porter Wagoner parted ways professionally, and we the public were provided all the details. The business of country music was, and still is, embedded in the city's culture.

What goes for Nashville was doubly true of Jerusalem. Even the leaders of this new, fledgling church could not find it in themselves to break from the culture that was so deeply implanted in the city's soil.

Maybe it had to do with the fact that he was not a native of Jerusalem, but once Paul left there to take the gospel of Christ to the Gentiles, he willingly gave up his allegiance to the old ways, leaving tradition-bound Jerusalem in his wake. Referring to his past orthodox attachment to the law, he says, "I regard everything as loss because of the surpassing value of knowing Christ Jesus my Lord" (Philippians 3:8). He saw the old Jewish ways as a hindrance to the free acceptance of the gospel, and defended vociferously the right of all, especially the Gentiles, not to have to obey them.

But once he was back in Jerusalem, Paul appears to have contradicted his own convictions. James, the brother of Jesus and the leader of the Jerusalem church, insists that Paul participate in what was called a Nazirite vow. And not only to participate in it, to pay for it! When a man made this vow, he went through what was called a rite of purification, primarily the shaving of one's head, along with a pledge to abstain from drinking wine and not to go near a human corpse. Once the head was shaved, a man's hair would not be cut again for a certain and prescribed period of time. It is quite possible that John the Baptist had once made such a vow.

And Paul did what James asked. It seems an odd thing for him to do, since it basically is a renunciation of what he has been proclaiming throughout his ministry to the Gentiles, that all these kinds of things are unnecessary once one gives his allegiance, his vow, to Jesus. If you know anything of Paul, you are aware that he could be as stubborn in his beliefs as anybody. But he gives in to James and makes the vow that James insists upon. The problem is, no one told his enemies, and it would not be long before a ruckus ensued and Paul would be taken into custody and hustled off to Rome and to his eventual death. Those who had cautioned him not to go to Jerusalem because of the danger there were correct.

Why did Paul do all this? Because he had made a vow to take an offering, received from the Gentile churches in the Mediterranean, to the destitute Jewish church in Jerusalem. And if Paul did nothing else, when he made a commitment—to Jesus or anybody—he kept his word.

It used to be, in our own culture, that a person's word and a handshake meant something. Not so much anymore, and perhaps that is why it is difficult for us to understand why it was so very important to Paul that he fulfill his responsibility in Jerusalem, and why Jacob requires Joseph to make his vow to him. What difference does it make where Jacob will be buried? He won't be around to argue about it!

FAVOR

Still, Jacob calls for Joseph and requires him to make his vow to his father yet again. "When I lie down with my ancestors, carry me out of Egypt and bury me in their burial place." And even when Joseph makes his promise once more, Jacob demands that he do it again for good measure, "Swear to me," he says, "swear to me." You can almost hear him in his near-death, gravelly voice, "Swear to me!" (Gen 47:30–31).

Death-bed promises carry a lot of emotional weight. A woman in our Florida congregation had died of throat cancer, and her service was conducted in a local chapel adjacent to the cemetery where her cremains were to be interred. In fact, her grave site was but a short walk from where the service took place. As her husband and I began making our way to the burial, while the other attendees waited, he stopped me and said he wanted to tell me about Jeanne's last moments of life. "She told me," he said, "that she didn't want me to get married again."

"Bob, you have to be kidding!" I responded. "That doesn't sound like Jeanne to me. Why, she was one of the most selfless women I've ever known. Besides, you're still a relatively young man with a lot of life ahead of you. I can't believe she would hold you to a promise like that!" He looked at me with a twinkle in his eye and said, "She told me just to go live with somebody!"

"Put your hand under my thigh and promise to deal loyally and truly with me," the dying Jacob says to his son (Gen 47:29). Another translation for dealing "loyally and truly" could be to "show kindness and faithfulness." The Hebrew word for "faithfulness" is *hesed*, a word we discussed previously. It represents a selfless devotion to someone else or a principle that is considered to be vital and unending. Evidently, Jacob is thinking not only of an appropriate resting place for himself, he is considering the promise that his birthright represents. He has twelve sons, and we know that from them will come a great nation. It is absolutely vital that the promise first given to Jacob's grandfather Abraham be fulfilled in those who come after him. And that fulfillment will not take place if the promise ends in Egypt.

We will be told in the Book of Exodus that one day there would emerge a Pharaoh who "knew not Joseph" (Exod 1:8). Jacob cannot, and will not, allow the destiny of his people finally to be in the hands of a foreigner who will not keep faith with the promise given to Abraham. His demand to be buried in Canaan is not selfish. He is thinking of all those who will come after him, carrying the blood that has come down through his grandfather and father, and continuing in the veins of the people who will commit themselves to the God who has claimed them.

When the Hebrews would identify themselves as the children of the God of Abraham, Isaac, and Jacob, it will be because they steadfastly continued the promise. They will have kept faith— *hesed*—with the God of their fathers. That is why Jacob demands to be buried in Canaan, next to his father and grandfather.

Are we keeping faith, you and I, not only with those who have come before us, but with those who will follow us? What is the level of our commitment to our faith, and what will those who come after us say of us when we have been, in a sense, buried with our fathers? The legacy we are forming in these days . . . will it last for all the time to come? It is a worthy question, don't you think? How will you choose this day to respond to it?

"I will do as you have said," Joseph says to his father Jacob. "I will do as you have said" (Gen 47:30).

When God asks a vow of loyalty of us, will we say the same?

Study/Thought Questions

1. Do you agree with the author that the progression of this narrative seems odd? If so, why?

2. Does Jacob not trust Joseph, or is it his way of assuring that God's purpose will be fulfilled?

3. Did Jacob ask a favor of Joseph or make a demand?

4. What did a vow mean in Jacob's day? What does it mean today?

5. Have you ever thought of Jacob as insecure?
6. Do you see a parallel in Jacob's experience with that of Paul's?
7. In demanding that his body be returned to Canaan, is Jacob thinking of the fulfillment of God's purpose that began with Abraham?
8. To what extent are you keeping faith . . . with those who came before you and those who will come after?

The Blessings of Your Father

"This is what their father said to them when he blessed them"
GENESIS 49:28

THE most difficult, and yet most satisfying task, of any pastor is to officiate a funeral. During my more than fifty years of pastoral service, I have led or participated in four hundred such events. That includes the funerals or memorial services of fifty couples, just since we came to live in Little Rock in 1996. My parents and my wife's parents are counted in that number.

Leading a funeral service is satisfying in that, if it is done well, family and friends of the deceased feel as if they have been well-served, not just by me but by the church I represent. My friend Bo Prosser has a well-known litany in regard to a church's ministry. He says it is done well when those who come to the church are "prepared for and cared for." At no time is that truer than when a loved one passes from this life to the next, and their church family does all within its power to see that such a transition is responded to in a caring and loving way. If that is indeed what happens, their loved one's life has been expressed in an appropriate fashion, and while it may not lessen their grief, they still feel as if the church has stood by them in their time of deepest need.

Any pastor, worth his or her salt, takes that responsibility very seriously.

The Blessings of Your Father

Officiating a funeral is also difficult. How is it possible, in just one worship service, to convey the essence of a person's entire life, especially one that has been lived long and well? What do you say to young parents when their small child has been taken from their arms? Is it possible to mask one's own feelings of anger and/or doubt when a young adult's life has been stolen away just as he or she is beginning to fly? How can you express in just a few words what the deceased has meant to those who have assembled to say their good-byes? I never feel so humbled or ill-prepared as when I sit down to consider what I might say and do for someone who has died.

Generally, when a death occurs, there is precious little time to prepare for such a thing. So if there is ever a need for the pastor to depend on the guiding Spirit of God, it is when he or she is preparing for a funeral. That is especially true when the pastor is also grieving. After having served my previous congregation several years, I confessed one Sunday in a sermon that I had been there long enough by that time that I no longer found myself conducting the funerals of church members; I was doing so for friends.

You can imagine that the greatest challenges I have faced in all my years of pastoral leadership have been when I led the funeral services for my parents and my wife's parents. When our daughter Emily announced to us that she wanted to get married, I immediately began thinking of how I would lead the wedding service. I was taken aback, and quite disappointed honestly, when she told me she didn't want me to do it. She just wanted me, on this sacred and holy occasion, to be her daddy.

I got over it.

I had no such luxury when it came to my parents' funerals. My brother Steve, who is a retired pastor, and I led both services, and quite frankly we did so because we just couldn't put them in the hands of someone else. The same was true when my wife's parents died. Her brother Gene, also a retired minister (our family members are getting old!) conducted their services.

Now that my days as an active pastor are over, what I miss most about the ministry is the funerals. There simply isn't any better way to reach down deeply into the souls of those who find themselves still living, and to make one's best effort in doing so is what I consider not only a great challenge but a high calling.

Looking at the story of Jacob's passing, it doesn't appear that his sons called in a priest to say words over him. Instead, it is Jacob who says the words himself. But he doesn't talk *about* himself. Before he takes his last breath, he blesses his sons, each and every one. Or, at least, that is what is written in the scriptures. Speaking of the twelve sons of Jacob, we are told, ". . . this is what their father said to them when he blessed them, blessing each one of them with a suitable blessing" (Gen 49:28).

Well, yes and no. Some of them received words of blessing and comfort, and others . . . not so much. Jacob, in poetic form, minces no words in letting his sons know what they could expect in the years that would come. If they had gotten the impression that during his lifetime, while mourning the loss of his son Joseph, their father Jacob had not been paying attention to their behavior, this death-bed scene should convince them that he had indeed kept a close eye on how they had conducted themselves—for the way they had lived thus far would mark the remainder of their days.

Joseph may have forgiven his brothers for throwing him into that pit and then selling him into slavery, but that doesn't mean that Jacob did. And it doesn't mean that Jacob forgot what they had done. We find him speaking to each of his sons . . .

Reuben, "unstable as water" (Gen 49:4) is the firstborn and the first to receive his father's "blessing." Simeon and Levi, along with Reuben and Judah the sons of Leah, are given to violence. In fact, Jacob would not have wanted to be in their council, he says, "for in their anger they killed men" (Gen 49:6). Say what you will about Jacob, but even with his checkered past he never resorted to violence. That doesn't mean, however, that some of his sons had not.

Zebulon shall live on the seashore and Issachar would find himself a slave, the victim of forced labor. Dan will become a judge, but will be like a viper waiting beside the road to bite the

The Blessings of Your Father

horse's heel, so that its rider falls backward. Gad will become a raider, Asher a cook for royalty, Naphtali like a doe that bears lovely fawns. Joseph and Judah, as we might expect, receive their father's greatest blessings while Benjamin, Jacob's youngest and the second son of Rachel's womb, surprisingly is depicted as a "ravenous wolf" (Gen 49:27).

In other words, if any of his sons—if any of us—expected old Jacob to get soft in his final hours and provide a reprieve to his boys because he knows he is about to leave them, we best think again.

And once he blesses his sons—in truth, he *characterizes* them—and the tribes that will come from their loins, Jacob again gives them their orders in regard to his burial. If he had not made it clear enough before, he will now with his final, dying breath. Jacob speaks to all his sons and tells them he is to be buried not in Egypt but in Canaan, next to his grandfather Abraham and his father Isaac.

Joseph has heard all this before. In fact, Jacob has made him swear that he will do as his father demands of him. But just in case something gets lost in translation or falls through the cracks, or for some reason the other brothers will try to overrule Joseph, Jacob repeats himself to all his sons. He will be buried in Canaan, not Egypt.

Understood? Good.

A lady in my previous congregation, a near relative, took Janet and me out to dinner. She was about to move to another city, she told us, to be near her son and his family in her declining years. "I don't care what anyone else in the family says," she told me. "When the time comes, I want *you* to do my funeral." A couple of weeks later she had a debilitating stroke, hastening the day when her funeral might come. When the time came, about a year later, for us to gather for her funeral, the occasion marked another couple whose funerals I have conducted.

Evidently, the old patriarch Jacob was sitting on the side of his bed, for when he finished telling his sons how to take care of him in death, he pulled his feet up under the covers, breathed his last, and as the narrative conveys it, "was gathered to his people" (Gen 49:33).

That's an interesting way of putting it, don't you think? Jacob "was gathered to his people." My friend John Killinger has said that "As we get older, our lives are filled with the ghosts of old friends and family members who have passed away. I don't think of this with sadness," he says. "On the contrary, it is wonderful and beautiful. It's as if our lives were literally crowded with the spirits of the people we've known and loved..."

He goes on to say, "I feel a solidarity with the dead—especially with my family members and former friends—that transcends the fact of their mortality. They are still a vital part of my life. Their love, their embraces, their words help to make me who I am today. Nothing as minor as physical death can separate us."[1]

And so, as he slips from this earth, Jacob finds himself surrounded by the presence of his grandfather Abraham, his father Isaac, and of course his beloved Rachel... even Leah, who Jacob was tricked into marrying, but was faithful to him and bore him four sons. It just goes to show that death-bed scenes, whether real or imagined, are fraught with emotion and drama.

Walter Wangerin, a Lutheran minister, tells of the time when, as a young boy, he and his family visited his mother's father in St. Louis. At first, he didn't understand why they were doing this, because it was in the middle of the school term, and his mother wasn't one for breaking the rules. So, obviously, this was not a vacation. Besides, as his mother was packing the family for the trip, she was short-tempered with him. There had to be a reason, a serious reason, for them to do such a thing. Soon he learned why they had traveled from Chicago to St. Louis to see the old man. They had gone there because his grandfather was dying of cancer.

Because of the man's illness, when he first saw him his grandson wasn't sure it was him. He didn't look like his grandpa.

"He rolled his head in my direction," Wangerin says. "He allowed his eyes to open, and he looked at me, and he said nothing at all, but he did this: he smiled."

1. Killinger, *Winter Soulstice*, 144–145.

The Blessings of Your Father

"I drew a sudden breath, and released it in a word: 'Grandpa,' I whispered. 'Grandpa, it's you.'"

"And then, without another word, he taught me what this dying is: and he taught me what you do for it. He invited me to himself. Having loved me when we walked the green and golden ground together, even now he disclosed the final mysteries to me, and he loved me to the end.

"The smile faded. Solemnly the old man raised his right hand from the sheets and reached in my direction. I understood the invitation. I knew what to do.

"I walked to him and stuck out my lesser hand. He took it and held it in his—and he did what you do for dying. We shook hands. He shook my little fist with a dignified, sober ceremony, first up, then down: Once. Twice.

"I learned. I did not tremble, and I did not cry, since I learned not only what you do for dying, but also what it is. It is leave-taking."[2]

There is no record of Jacob shaking the hands of his sons. Instead, he speaks sternly and forthrightly to them of what their lives will continue to yield, providing a clear picture of the way the nation of Israel would be, the people who would come from the loins of Abraham, Isaac, and Jacob, and Jacob's sons, the people named after this old, irascible patriarch, Israel, the name given him by God. But in his own, hard-bitten, stubborn, unique way, Jacob blesses his sons. In the only way he knows how, Jacob blesses his sons. It is his way of leave-taking.

All of us, I would think, would like to have the blessing of our fathers—and mothers!—upon their passing and long before. That is not always the case, of course, but now would be the time for us, you and me, to assure that when it comes to those who follow us, children or otherwise, they receive our blessing while we still have breath to give it.

I can't think of anyone, certainly myself included, who has not been blessed far, far beyond anything we deserve. We do indeed run into trouble when we think somehow that for whatever

2. Wangerin., *Miz Lil*, 21–22.

reason we *do* deserve it. So let us understand that the only thing we are supposed to do, when it comes to blessings, blessings we have not earned—those given to us by God or by others we have come to know—is to give them away to those we meet.

When was the last time you blessed someone? Don't tell me you don't know how to do that because you do. Sometimes it's nothing more than a smile. At other times, it is a kind word, perhaps a thoughtful note or card, the willingness to help someone with no strings attached. But whatever we do, and whenever or however we do it, blessings find their origins in the grace of God.

He applies it to Moses, but what John Claypool says is just as true of old, dying Jacob. He speaks of "a subtle reminder of how mysterious and ingenious are God's ways of taking bad things and turning them to good advantage." And then, in classic Claypool terminology, he says, "In the hands of this alchemist God of Holy Scripture, nothing is ever wasted, and the lead of difficult experiences is often turned into the gold of blessing."[3]

Let Jacob's story, and Joseph's, and the example of Jacob's other sons, illustrate for us clearly that we do not deserve the grace God bestows upon us. But having received such a blessing, we are called upon to share it with others. I remind you, Jacob, in using his last breath to speak to his sons, "blessed them," blessed "each one of them with a suitable blessing."

If nothing else, we, you and I, should feel that we are suitably blessed with the grace bestowed on us by the God of Abraham, Isaac, and Jacob—and, of course, Jesus.

As Jacob repeated his desire not to be buried in Egypt but to be returned to his beloved Canaan, let us repeat this: when we acknowledge and receive God's blessing, let us commit ourselves to imparting that blessing to others. It is the only way to share in God's presence wherever we are.

---

3. Claypool, *Hopeful Heart*, 48.

Study/Thought Questions

1. As difficult as it may be, reflect upon the passing of your loved ones. What impact did it have on you at the time? What impact does it have on you now?
2. Were Jacob's final words to his sons truly a blessing, or were they simply a depiction of the way their lives would be spent? In other words, is this hindsight on the part of the narrative's author?
3. Did Jacob forgive his sons for what they did to Joseph?
4. The narrative says that upon his death Jacob was "gathered to his people." How does that inform your theological understanding of the after-life?
5. How do you think of death as "leave-taking"?
6. Who has blessed you, in word and deed? How do you hope to pass that blessing on to others?
7. Do you agree with the author that blessings find their origins in the grace of God?
8. What do you make of John Claypool's affirmation that in the hands of God nothing is ever wasted?

Intentions

"What if Joseph still bears a grudge . . . ?"

ᴄ❧ GENESIS 50:15 ☙ᴅ

WHEN it comes to the story of Joseph, Frederick Buechner says the final chapter of Genesis, when once again Joseph has a confrontation with his brothers, is the "real moment of truth."[1] Everything we have witnessed in Joseph's life thus far leads to this encounter when the brothers come to him and ask his forgiveness and mercy. Father Jacob, the old Hebrew patriarch, last in the original line of those who initiated and formed the faith, has gone to his eternal resting place with his fathers. His passing unleashes all manner of guilt and fear on the part of his sons; that is, on the part of his sons who are not Joseph. We can understand how they must feel. After all, Joseph now has the upper hand.

They are in Egypt because of the famine. They have stayed in Egypt because of Joseph's ability to provide for them. It is in Egypt that the family of Jacob "were fruitful and multiplied exceedingly." The famine now lies twelve years in the dust of time. Prosperity and fruitfulness have replaced the despair that came during those years when the land produced no grain.

But it is obvious that, though Joseph is responsible for all the good fortune they have had since settling in Egypt, it is Jacob—it

---

1. Buechner, 78.

INTENTIONS

is still and always has been Jacob—who has held the family together . . . which is rather ironic when you stop and think about Jacob's checkered past. Wasn't Jacob the one who caused the rupture of his father's family by stealing his brother's birthright, forcing him to have to run away for years and be separated from his family? Wasn't it Jacob who took flight from his father-in-law Laban, not only taking Laban's daughters from him but his gods as well? Somewhere along the way, Jacob evidently has managed to put his spurious past behind him and become the patriarch, the head of the family he was always meant to be—for Jacob is now Israel, the father of a nation.

And now that Jacob lies with his ancestors, the brothers fear that the family's fortunes and future will come to an abrupt end. It is quite possible, to their way of thinking, that Joseph might take advantage of the situation and bring down retribution upon them for the way they treated him so many years before.

If indeed there would come a time when a pharaoh arose who "knew not Joseph" (Exod 1:8), he's got nothing on Joseph's very own brothers. They don't seem to know him at all.

But it's not the first time such a thing has occurred, and chances are it won't be the last. I've seen it before, and possibly so have you . . . the head of the family dies and relationships and behaviors start to unravel. It seems there's always someone in the family who, despite the fragility of relationships, holds things together. And when the "glue" is gone, things fall apart.

When my father died, a good friend from my childhood looked at me and with a sardonic grin on his face, said, "Well, Hyde, you're now the last line of defense." He knew of which he spoke because he had gone through such an experience himself when his father died years before. Sometimes, the "last line of defense" does not hold, is ineffective in the face of an all-out blitz, and the family starts to disintegrate. Is that going to happen in the house of Jacob, now that the old rascal is gone?

Hasn't enough time passed that the sons of Jacob should have come to understand and know their brother Joseph, to see that his motives are clear and his integrity, not to mention his love, toward them runs deep? Hasn't seventeen years been enough time for them to learn the heart of their brother so they might trust him and his intentions? Evidently not.

And what is it about the number seventeen? Joseph was seventeen when he started telling his brothers and their father about his wild and crazy dreams. He was seventeen when Jacob, obviously loving Joseph best, gives him that fancy coat. He was seventeen when they threw him in the pit and then sold him into slavery. And now, they've been in Egypt seventeen years, a dozen past the end of the famine, and it is for them a time of reckoning, or as Buechner says, the "moment of truth."

What do you think caused the brothers of Joseph to be so suspicious of his motives, thinking that he might turn on them once Jacob was dead and buried? Hasn't he been generous to them? Hasn't he saved them from certain death? Hasn't Joseph bent over backwards to accommodate his siblings, their families, their needs? Why do you think they responded to Joseph the way they did once Jacob is buried back home in Canaan?

Apparently, it was guilt over what they had done to him so many years before. William Sloane Coffin says that "the worst form of psychological pain is the guilt that comes from sin."[2] But what is the source of the sin that leads to guilt? Usually, it is some form of deception.

We can understand their jealousy to a certain extent. We might possibly have felt the same way. The scriptures make it clear that Jacob favored Joseph, proving that the old trickster was not exactly up for the Jaycees' *Father of the Year Award*. I'm sure we would all agree that no one wins in a family when one child is favored over the others.

We can relate to the anger that resulted from their situation. As we have pointed out, even Jacob was upset when Joseph came to them with his dream that one day his brothers and his father would bow down before him. That Joseph was eventually right about that does nothing to take away from the moment when the

---

2. Coffin, *Credo*, 16.

entire house of Jacob is seething at Joseph's arrogance and immaturity. No doubt, we would have been angry too.

It could be that the brothers remember Joseph's dreams and have faced the startling reality that his dreams are now being realized. They *have* bowed down before him. They could not have survived without him, and certainly could not have prospered without his great generosity toward them. The brothers are beholden, and as the sons of a patriarch that could have been a very uncomfortable place for them to be.

Jealousy can be overcome. Anger can be forgotten. Humility can be dealt with. But guilt—long-lasting, burning, deeply-rooted guilt—is usually the result of a heart that has not been forgiven its past deception. And there was plenty of that in Jacob's household. The sons come back from Dothan with Joseph's bloody coat, telling their father that their little brother has been attacked and killed by a wild animal. Jacob might have suspicioned that they were lying to him, but under the circumstances he has no recourse but to believe them.

Again we turn to G. Henton Davies, who says pointedly that "Liars rarely trust others."[3] Jacob obviously forgave his sons for their deception. Isn't it true that those who have been forgiven much are that much more willing to forgive? Certainly, Jacob knew what it meant to receive such forgiveness. But that doesn't mean his sons have been able to forget their own sin and the resulting guilt. And now that Daddy is gone, "What if Joseph still bears a grudge against us . . . " they ask one another (Gen 50:15).

Say what you will about the brothers of Joseph, but they don't leave it alone to fester. They deal with the situation in which they find themselves. They take the bull by the horns and seek a resolution. It may have to do with their basic desire for survival, but whatever the motivation might have been, give them credit for this: they go to the source and deal with Joseph on an intentional level. They don't leave the situation to get worse on its own. Deal with it and face the consequences.

It was the right thing, the most redemptive thing, to do.

3. Davies, *Broadman Bible Commentary*, 302.

Dream Catcher

Still, there's a sense in which they hide behind the skirts of their father's robe by invoking Jacob's dying wish. They relay Jacob's message to Joseph: " . . . forgive the crime of your brothers and the wrong they did in harming you." And if the point wasn't made clear the first time, they repeat it. This time they say *please*. "Now therefore *please* forgive the crime of the servants of the God of your father" (Gen 50:17).

Once again, Joseph's long-ago dream comes true. His brothers are bowing prostrate at his feet. My guess is that this gave more satisfaction to the storyteller than it did to Joseph. I doubt that Joseph felt any gratification for the fact that his long-ago dream has come true, though it is also doubtful he had forgotten it. Quite frankly, with the passing of time—not to mention the passing of their father Jacob—it hardly seems important anymore. Knowing that the future of the nation called Israel lies in the balance, Joseph's intention is a full and lasting reconciliation with his brothers. And that is far more important than his being able to tell them, "I told you so!"

That reconciliation has come about because Joseph has taught his brothers a great lesson: faith overcomes all circumstances, all jealousies, all anger, all fear, all guilt. This is the way Denise Levertov depicts faith, which certainly applies to the faith of Joseph:

> *As swimmers dare*
> *to lie face to the sky*
> *and water bears them,*
> *as hawks rest upon air*
> *and air sustains them;*
> *so would I learn to attain*
> *freefall, and float*
> *into Creator Spirit's deep embrace,*
> *knowing no effort earns*
> *that all-surrounding grace.*[4]

The heart of this encounter has to do with Joseph's response. Through his tears, he informs his brothers that only God can truly forgive, and as powerful and influential as he might be in the land

---

4. Borg, *Childish Things*, 331.

INTENTIONS

of Egypt, Joseph is not God. To the contrary, he could not have managed the roller-coaster experiences of all the years had it not been for his God who had been with him.

With that in mind, he throws a little theology at them. "Even though you intended to do harm to me," he says (notice how he still gets in a bit of a dig at them), "God intended it for good, in order to preserve a numerous people, as he is doing today" (Gen 50:20).

Frankly, whenever I hear anyone, even Joseph, start speaking for God (which he clearly does here, even though he has told his brothers he has no intention to be put in God's place), I get a little nervous. In Joseph's view of things, does he believe God saw what would transpire over the years, so God did this, manipulated that, in order for God's purpose to be done? Once a pharaoh emerged who knew not Joseph, and the Israelites suffered four centuries of slavery before being liberated at the hands of Moses, did God maneuver all those occurrences—make God's people suffer—so they would eventually find themselves in the Promised Land where God intended them to be all along? Before you answer that question, think long and hard. Do you really want to answer for God?

And do you want to know what I think? I think the one who wrote this story years later looks back on what did occur after the Israelites came to Egypt—with their subsequent wanderings in the wilderness and their eventual conquering of Canaan—and interpreted why and how it all came about. Okay, I'll go so far as to say that the narrator of this account of Joseph may very well have put these words in Joseph's mouth.

Now, before you react to that, consider that we do the very same thing every time we gather for worship. We put words, thoughts, and deeds into God's mouth, not to mention God's heart, God's intention. We often invoke the words of the psalmists. Look carefully at the hymns that were used by the Israelites, and you will find plenty of examples where God is spoken for by those who led worship. We do the same by looking back and interpreting where we've been and what it means, choosing to find in our past how and where God has been with us. So when you think about it, you can't help but realize that it is an act of faith to do such a thing.

If we are not so bold as to speak for God, like the sons of Jacob all we are left with is our jealousy, our anger, and our guilt. It is in the interpretation of our respective and collective journeys of faith—in other words, our attempts to speak for God—that we find the impetus to go on, if for no other reason than it takes great faith to do so.

As did Joseph, we speak for God, you and I, in everything we do. Sometimes we do so with words, more often with deeds. The eternally important thing for us to consider is that when we do, we ask God to intend it for good.

May it ever be so. May it ever be so.

Study/Thought Questions

1. How has Jacob's death caused Joseph's brothers to be fearful?

2. The author says it is ironic, given Jacob's checkered past, that he was viewed as the glue that held his family together. Do you agree? Who is the one person in your family serving in such a role?

3. In light of this portion of the narrative, do the brothers of Joseph still not trust him?

4. Has there ever been a "moment of truth" (Buechner) in your family? If so, when?

5. The author draws a correlation between guilt and deception. Do you agree?

6. Are the brothers starting finally to realize that Joseph's dreams, as a young man, are being realized? Is this their way of responding to that?

7. Guilt can be forgiven, perhaps, but can it be overcome?

8. Reconciliation seems to be Joseph's purpose. Is it yours?

INTENTIONS

9. Do you agree with the author that the one who wrote this narrative put words into Joseph's mouth? Ultimately, does it really matter?

10. The author says that looking back on our respective faith journeys, and interpreting God's intention in them, is an act of faith. Do you agree?

11. Now that we have considered the whole of Joseph's life, what is the singular, most important lesson this narrative has taught you?

Bibliography

Borg, Marcus. *Putting Away Childish Things*. New York: HarperOne, 2010.
Brueggemann, Walter. *Genesis: Interpretation: A Bible Commentary for Teaching and Preaching*. Edited by James Luther Mays. Atlanta: John Knox, 1982.
Buechner, Frederick. *Peculiar Treasures*. New York: Harper & Row, 1979.
Cartledge, Tony. "Selling Joseph." *Nurturing Faith*. July–August 2017, 34 and 36.
Claypool, John. *The Hopeful Heart*. Harrisburg, Pennsylvania: Morehouse, 2003.
Coffin, William Sloane. *Credo*. Louisville: Westminster John Knox, 2004.
Davies, G. Henton. *The Broadman Bible Commentary, Volume 1*. Edited by Clifton J. Allen. Nashville: Broadman, 1969.
Francisco, Clyde T. *The Broadman Bible Commentary, Volume 1 Revised*. Edited by Clifton J. Allen. Nashville: Broadman, 1969.
Fretheim, Terence E. *The New Interpreter's Bible, Volume I*. Edited by Leander E. Keck. Nashville: Abingdon, 1994.
https://bluefeatherspirit.wordpress.com
Killinger, John R. *Winter Soulstice*. New York: Crossroad, 2005.
Marty, Peter W. *Christian Century*. "Make Today Great Again." *Christian Century*, October 26, 2016, 3.
Swindoll, Charles R. and Lee Hough. *Joseph: From Pit to Pinnacle*. Dallas: Word, 1990.
Taylor, Barbara Brown. *An Altar in the World*. New York: HarperOne, 2009.
———. *Gospel Medicine*. Cambridge, Massachusetts: Cowley, 1995.
Von Rad, Gerhard, *Genesis*. Philadelphia: Westminster, 1961.
Wangerin, Walter, Jr. *Miz Lil & The Chronicles of Grace*. San Francisco: Harper & Row, 1988.